HITLERISM
— *die Endlösung* —

Martin Friedrich

BOOKS FROM CLEMENS & BLAIR
— www.clemensandblair.com —

Hitler Avatāra, by Martin Friedrich
Sin Against the Blood, by Artur Dinter
Protocols of the Elders of Zion, edited by Thomas Dalton
The Riddle of the Jews' Success, by Theodor Fritsch
Triumph of the Truth, by Robert Penman
The Book of the Shulchan Aruch, by Erich Bischoff
For My Legionnaires, by Corneliu Codreanu
Myth and Sun, by Martin Friedrich
Unmasking Anne Frank, by Ikuo Suzuki
Pan-Judah! Political Cartoons of Der Stürmer, by Robert Penman
Passovers of Blood, by Ariel Toaff
The Poisonous Mushroom, by Ernst Hiemer
On the Jews and Their Lies, by Martin Luther
Mein Kampf, by Adolf Hitler
Mein Kampf (Dual English-German edition), by Adolf Hitler
The Essential Mein Kampf, by Adolf Hitler
The Myth of the 20th Century, by Alfred Rosenberg

BOOKS BY THOMAS DALTON
— www.thomasdaltonphd.com —

The Steep Climb: Essays on the Jewish Question
Classic Essays on the Jewish Question: 1850 to 1945
Debating the Holocaust
The Holocaust: An Introduction
The Jewish Hand in the World Wars
Eternal Strangers: Critical Views of Jews and Judaism
Hitler on the Jews
Goebbels on the Jews
Streicher, Rosenberg, and the Jews: The Nuremberg Transcripts

HITLERISM
— *die Endlösung* —

Martin Friedrich

Clemens & Blair, LLC
— 2024 —

CLEMENS & BLAIR, LLC

Copyright © 2024 Martin Friedrich
Foreword copyright © 2024, by Thomas Dalton

All rights reserved. No part of this publication may be reproduced, stored in a retrieval system, or transmitted, in any form or by any means, electronic, mechanical, photocopying, recording, or otherwise.

Clemens & Blair, LLC, is a non-profit educational publisher.
www.clemensandblair.com

Library of Congress Cataloging-in-Publication Data

Friedrich, Martin
Hitlerism: die Endlösung

p. cm.
Includes bibliographical references

ISBN 979-8987-7263-96
(hbk.: alk. paper)

1. Hitlerism
2. Hitler, Adolf
3. National Socialism

Printing number: 9 8 7 6 5 4 3 2 1

Printed in the United States of America on acid-free paper.

For the fighters:
You are not dead.
You are not caged.
You are not forgotten.

The light on the horizon is an end.
It is our Fury and silhouettes the Enemy.
Beyond it sits the mystery of all beginning.

As a man of mere intellect, the Jew stands aloof from national ties; the Jew has no country. He assures the proletarians that they have no country either. He persuades them that there is no such thing as a unity of land and nation; that the only tie between men is economic interest and that this tie unites them with the global proletariat. The Jew means to rob the working classes of all those values which are theirs by birthright; values which have been won for them by their ancestors, and which are their inheritance also.
— Arthur Möller van den Bruck
Das Dritte Reich, 1923

Nothing is here for tears, nothing to wail
  Or knock the breast, no weakness, no contempt,
Dispraise, or blame, nothing but well and fair,
  And what may quiet us in a death so noble.
— John Milton
Samson Agonistes

Who will condemn the hatred of evil that springs from the love of what is good and just? ... If you love your people, you cannot but hate the enemies that compass their destruction...
— Menachem Begin, Prime Minister of Israel
The Revolt, 1951

Contents

FOREWORD by Thomas Dalton	i
Revelations: A Preface	1
1: Accelerationism and the Judeo-System	15
2: Population and Technics	59
3: The Figurative World	95
Afterword	131
Bibliography	145

Foreword
Thomas Dalton

At the present time, humanity faces three dramatic problems: runaway technology, human population (growth and movement), and global Jewry. Any one of these could mean our end; all three at once practically guarantee a catastrophe of the highest magnitude.

Of particular interest is the Jewish hand in technology and population questions. As we speak, powerful and influential Jews are working hard to develop technologies that could quickly exceed human grasp and control, and that could be horribly misused by malevolent actors around the world. One need only ponder the more prominent names — Zuckerberg, Brin, Page, Ellison, Dell, Mosseri, Wojcicki, Altman, Jassy — to realize that Jews are front-and-center in the most pervasive, most dangerous, and most potent technologies. Super-AI, intelligent and autonomous drones, advanced robotics, and nanotechnologies all present multiple disaster scenarios that could eliminate literally billions of people; and their future development works at the behest of a handful of wealthy Jews.

So too on the population front: Jews in the US and Europe lead the way in open-border policies, Third-World immigration, multiracial societies, racial mixing, and so-called minority rights. They do their best to stifle open debate on these issues, and they work to ensure that there is no substantive discussion on global overpopulation. With perhaps the exception of abortion, Jews are inevitably in favor of population growth — more people mean more consumers, more taxpayers, more soldiers, and more fodder for Jewish machinations.

The glib critic may say, "Look, no need to worry about a tech disaster; if that strikes, it will solve our population problem!" This is a bad joke at best. To allow booming (and mixing) populations while awaiting technological Armageddon is sheer idiocy; it is the worst, most torturous form of collective suicide that one might imagine. And yet this is precisely the future that global Jewry is marching us toward.

∞ ∞ ∞

One hundred years ago, certain Europeans had bad feelings about just such issues. Naturally, the specific forms of their concerns were unique to their day; the technology and the population questions of 1920 presented less-pressing problems than they do now. But the Jewish threat, interestingly, was as severe as ever. As far back as 1850, composer Richard Wagner was decrying Jewish infiltration and commodification of the art and music scene in Europe. By the 1870s, writers could issue well-argued pamphlets on "the conquest of the world by the Jews" and "the victory of Jewry over Germandom." By the 1880s, Jews controlled roughly half of the wealth on the Continent. By the 1890s, German journalist and businessman Theodor Fritsch could publish a concise summary of the dire social ills wrought by Jewry:

> The Jewish register of sins is briefly as follows: The Jews constitute, under the guise of a 'religion,' a political, social, and commercial fraternity that, directed by similar instincts and in a secret agreement within itself, operates towards the exploitation and subjugation of the non-Jewish peoples. The Jews of all countries and all languages are united in this goal and cooperate among themselves towards it...
>
> In his separate community, the Jew considers all non-Jews as his enemies whom he has to combat with cunning and treachery. Through his special moral laws, the Talmud and the Shulchan Aruch, the Jew considers himself as standing outside all other legal prescriptions and considers himself justified in violating all national laws — but always in such a way that this abuse cannot be proven in him. On the basis of the Talmudic view of life that grants the name of 'man' only to the Jew and counts the other peoples as animals, the Jew is exempted from every feeling of duty and any conscience with regard to the other peoples. Talmudic moral doctrine justifies him to commit every lie and deception towards mankind

— although he is required to do so in such a way as to avoid any retribution via the letter of the public law...

Another spur to Jewish efforts is found in the superstitious 'promises' of the ancient Jewish scriptures: "All nations shall serve you and you shall be a lord above all thy brothers," "You shall consume all nations," etc. The Jews, in their arrogance, consider themselves the 'natural aristocracy' of mankind and think that they must, as such, actually strive for the mastery of the world.

But since they cannot do this at all through bravery and truly superior strength, they attempt it through lies and deception — and money. Jewry thinks that it has recognized as the final wisdom of the world the fact that "money rules the world." Jewry thinks that one who has money is the natural ruler of the world. The Jews therefore do not reject any means and ways to amass money. Every deception and treachery that leads to enrichment seems therefore to be, in their eyes, not only permissible but commanded and blessed! In this way, usury, robbery, false bankruptcy, etc. seem to them to be harmless activities. They consider every lie, every betrayal, every perjury as justified if they lead to an advantage for themselves.[1]

It was precisely in such an environment that a young Adolf Hitler first became politically active and first developed his vision for his Germanic people: his philosophy of life, that which we would come to call *Hitlerism*. By all accounts, Hitler was a man of the people and for the people. He fought against the Jewish criminals that cost Germany the First World War; he fought against Jewish domination and manipulation in the Weimar regime; and he worked always for the betterment, and the spiritual enhancement, of the common man.

By the time he wrote *Mein Kampf* in the mid-1920s, Hitler had worked out the key elements of his philosophy:

---

[1] Cited from "Questions and Answers" in Thomas Dalton, ed., *Classic Essays on the Jewish Question* (2022), 200-201.

- The worker and the farmer are the foundation of society and must be defended.
- Modern, large cities are functional and moral cesspools, especially when under Jewish influence.
- A growing German population must have land on which to live and farm.
- The German population must remain racially uncontaminated — unlike the bastardized and "niggerized" French, for example.
- The Germanic, Nordic, and Aryan peoples are the true source of social and cultural greatness.
- The Jew poses the single greatest direct threat to social well-being.

But perhaps Hitler's most fundamental insight was this: *Life is perpetual struggle.* Society must struggle against the loafers, the parasites, the dreck; and individuals must struggle against apathy, sloth, defeatism, and complacency. No person, nor any nation, must rest on its laurels, or surrender to luxury and comfort. To give up the struggle is to give up on life, and on the future. *To surrender the future* — this is the great danger of the modern age. Hitler surely would have opposed anything, any modern technologies or conveniences, that tended toward inaction or softness.

But the greatest struggle, then as now, was the Jew. Hitler's Germany faced Jewish threats on three fronts simultaneously: to the East, in Judeo-Bolshevik Russia; to the West, in Judeo-capitalist England and France; and internally, in the German-Jewish population that was determined to corrupt and degrade the nation. Such a situation would have been insurmountable for most. But Hitler realized that all was not lost, that the depth and power of the Aryan soul could, under the right conditions, reemerge and triumph over the oriental Hebraic invaders. Thus he mapped out a road to power that would be realized in less than a decade (in 1933), and which would, in just six more years, raise up the German nation to global heights.

But to do this, he knew he would have to confront and defeat the Jew. This would mean: identifying him, naming him, shaming him, encouraging him to leave, and ultimately, forcing him to leave. It was, in essence, not a complicated vision or plan; rather, it was essentially simple: *identify the Jew and drive him out*. This alone would be a great success, and would lead to other successes in virtually every area of life.

∞ ∞ ∞

Hitler was obviously not the first to strive for spiritual greatness among his people. The ancient Greeks — Socrates, Plato, and Aristotle, and before them, Homer — held such a vision for their beloved Hellas. The great writers of the major European cultures promoted it: Cicero, Dante Alighieri, Voltaire, Shakespeare, and Goethe. In Germany, Schopenhauer and especially Nietzsche wrote with a tremendous potency and insight. These men achieved much; but vitally, they never *led*. They were never in a position to craft a future for their people, and then to *see it through to realization*. Hitler was not primarily a writer, but in voice and vision, he equaled or exceeded these great men of the past. He could lead a military, lead a national government, and serve as a spiritual inspiration for millions; who in history can claim such achievements?

Yes, we know that he lost the war, and that he sacrificed his own life. Himmler, Göring, and Goebbels did the same. But death is not defeat. Death comes to all. What matters is that Hitler was unbowed to the end, that he never capitulated, never gave up. Even when confronted with the combined might of much of the industrial world, and facing near-certain defeat, he pressed on. He lost the war; he lost his life; but there is no disgrace in that. In fact, just the opposite: in fighting to the end, under impossible conditions, he served as the greatest possible role model for the future.

For Hitler, the Aryan people have a great destiny in this world — a divine destiny and a spiritual mission. There will be much resistance along the way; there will be death and defeat; *nonetheless*, he said, we must press on. We may be crushed in the process of the fight; *nonetheless*, we must persevere. *This* is the "philosophy of nonetheless." *This* is Hitlerism.

∞ ∞ ∞

We all know the history of great deeds and great thoughts. But who can take on the mantle and articulate these ideas in the present day? I can think of no better man than Martin Friedrich. His many years of thought and writing have sharpened his skills like no other. He wields his pen like a saber. As a master swordsman, Friedrich shreds the superficial and weak ideas that surround Hitler and his National Socialism. In their place, he crafts a powerful and poetic text in defense of Hitlerism — one that is as intellectually sound as it is emotionally and spiritually moving.

His prior works, and especially his books *Myth and Sun* and *Hitler Avatāra*, establish him as among the foremost poet-writers on Hitlerism. He follows in the large footsteps of Nietzsche and Serrano, but he does them justice. Every generation produces but a few men who are able to write with such power and conviction, and we are fortunate to have Friedrich on our side, working on behalf of Eternal Justice and calling us to battle.

As I read the following text, I am reminded of a short sonnet by the Canadian poetess Ethelwyn Wetherald called "My Orders." She deeply understood the call-to-arms:

> *My orders are to fight;*
> *Then if I bleed, or fail,*
> *Or strongly win, what matters it?*
> *God only doth prevail.*
>
> *The servant craveth naught*
> *Except to serve with might.*
> *I was not told to win or lose,–*
> *My orders are to fight.*

Aryan! Your orders are to fight! Whether you personally prevail means nothing; many are destined to fall. But if *the Aryan* fights, *the Aryan* will win. Fighting *is* winning. The Aryan is a force of Nature, and Nature, in the long run, always prevails. This, it seems to me, is the essence of Hitlerism.

Don't curse your fate, Aryan. Praise it. It is a blessing. It is an honor and a privilege to live in a time of great battles. When World War One broke out, the 25-year-old Hitler was elated: "I sank down on my knees and thanked heaven, out of the fullness of my heart, for the good fortune of living at such a time." He desperately sought to prove that his feeling for his fellow Germans was not mere talk, not meaningless platitudes. In great struggles, "the Goddess of Destiny's inexorable hand tests the truth and sincerity of nations and men." Now, Hitler could "appear before the Court of Eternal Justice and testify to the truth" of his feelings. Upon his acceptance into the Bavarian military, he experienced "indescribable joy"; later in life, he often looked back on "those early weeks of war, when kind Fate allowed me to take my place in that heroic struggle among the nations."[2]

Aryans — the battle is underway! You are all accepted! Kind Fate has allowed you all to take part. Fall down on your knees and swear allegiance to your fellow men. Thank the heavens. Take up the fight. The gods are with us. The anti-race has played itself out once again; its crimes are now open for all to see. The Goddess of Inexorable Vengeance is preparing to redress the treason of millennia.[3] She calls on you for help.

Let me leave the last word to Arthur Schopenhauer. In this world of struggle and strife, of conflict and loss, of pain and death, happiness is largely an illusion. For the most part, the "happy ones" today are those who have disengaged from the great struggles, thus acquiring a temporary respite, but only at the cost of widespread social decay. Short-term "happiness" leads only to long-term pain. Therefore, says Schopenhauer, "a happy life is impossible." Do not strive for that. What then to do? He tells us:

---

[2] *Mein Kampf*, volume 1, sections 5.2 and 5.3, 321-325.
[3] Cf. *Mein Kampf*, volume 1, section 12.22, 675.

> The best that man can attain is a *heroic life*, such as is lived by one who struggles against overwhelming odds in some way and in some affair that will benefit the whole of mankind, and who, in the end, triumphs — although he obtains a poor reward, or none at all.[4]

Aryans, you are called upon to be heroes. The personal reward will be slight or nonexistent. But it will put you on a path to greatness. Heroes are never forgotten. Their deeds live on. Thus, strive for greatness. Engage in the great battle. You are needed now more than ever.

---

[4] *Parerga and Paralipomena* (1974), volume 2, section 172a, 322.

— Revelations —
A Preface

> *Ours is the faith that promises victory if only we are fanatical enough.*
>
> — Adolf Hitler
> 01 May 1923

1.

Hitlerism is the philosophy of *nonetheless*. This philosophy consists of doing what's right in the face of insurmountable odds — not for material gain, but for communion and reconciliation with God.

The Hitlerist understands *God* to be that which *stands for* quality and decency and *stands against* the rising tide of mass depravity, which threatens to undermine Eternal Nature. God is the transcendent will of a divinely inspired folk. The Aryan God is the Aryan will. The Hitlerist absolutely rejects the Judeo-Christian Satan-Jehovah — for all time.

What is right is what is good: "the Good is that which transcends and uplifts; it is sacrificing oneself for the benefit of the whole that reflects oneself; this reflection is physical, mental, and spiritual; the Good is one thing. The Good is the blood in your veins that both does and does not belong to you."[1]

Hitlerism is a creed of faith — "not a faith of the meek, but that of the strong and noble."[2] It is not a doctrine with the selfish aim of material gain. By doing what is right and good — by *sacrificing oneself for the benefit of the whole that reflects oneself* — selfish *material gain* becomes only a byword for those destined to fail. This is not to say that Hitlerism has no worldly goals, for it seeks the restoration of God and Nature. But in their form, content, establishment, and resolution, these objectives are distinct from that which can be tied to selfish, material gain — e.g., the materiality of politics. The restoration of God and Nature means breaking with the deification of material for good and all; it means communion with the transcendent for the elevation of spirit and ultimate downfall of that which reduces spirit.

As a creed of faith, Hitlerism is the most fanatical fanaticism. There is no more divine cause than God, no worthier goal than Nature. These ends are sought because they *edify* man and, moreover, are the only means of *defining* man in an age of crass politicking. "We are ... fanatics, not dancers on the tight-rope of moderation!" With this, Adolf Hitler avowed his goal: embrace meaning to the point of self-sacrifice.[3] This meaning is both creation and destruction, it is *faith* and *deed*: it is creation of a will that seeks the transcendent (family, kin, clan, culture — i.e., *God-in-man*); it is destruction of a system that suppresses or precludes the creation and exercise of the *God-in-man*, which is the will to act.

In this age of politicking, this age of material-man and his exploitative *gaining*, in this Age of the Jew and its gofer-goyim, there is no higher call than the sacrificial sanctity of Hitlerist faith — for it will take a fanatic willing to forfeit everything tied to the Judeo-system to disrupt the system whose own fanatical aim is the devastation of man, Nature, and God.

Hitlerism is absolute duty to God.

Absolute means *uncompromising*; therefore *politicking*, crass *material-mindedness* — or that which is predicated on compromise — is *inconceivable*. The absolute is *uncorrupted-ness*, it is *purity*, and purity of heart is to *will one thing*.[4] "The worldly goal," the material goal, on the other hand, "is not one thing in its essence because it is *unreal*. Its so-called unity is actually nothing but *emptiness* which is hidden beneath the *manyness*."[5] Conversely, the *real* one thing is the Good, which demands, if *we* are good, all our attention and effort. And what is this *one thing* if not the holy call of *transcendence* — transcendence of the self for the Eternal?

Duty is the binding call of self-sacrifice; it is the ultimate tautology: *what ought to be done is what ought to be done*, and it is done *absolutely*, without compromise, in purity, and for the sake of those who came before and for those yet to come. When, during the great Kurukshetra War, Arjuna hesitated on the battlefield, concerned over the devastation soon to be unleashed, he heard the whisper of eternity through Krishna Avatāra: it was Govinda, the supreme Cause of Causes. Govinda compels the dutiful man to fulfill his being and thus fulfill his meaning: you exist to continue the arc of God on earth; the Cause of Causes is the cause of the faithful to surmount the insurmountable, to grapple with the anguished calls of those sacrificed on the battlefield. *Yes*, the faithful yearn for *more*, for the faithful are part of the sacrifice fulfilling God's will on earth. Arjuna hesitated because he was tempted by a lesser will: man's *will-to-materiality*. Arjuna became a legend because he fulfilled a higher will: God's *will-to-eternity*, the Eternal Arc. When you stand judged beyond all time and space, there is one measure that seals your fate: faith, for *eternity asks solely about faithfulness.*[6]

It is by fulfilling our duty that we are reconciled with God. And through this communion of finite and infinite, the *God who is* becomes more than the *God who was*.[7] For the sacrificial act of incarnation of divine will on earth impresses on God the mark of man, who must live, fight, and die with honor and loyalty to overcome the demiurgic stain of godless materiality. Through the heroic struggle of the Aryan, who knows "the value of life ... [which is] based on spiritual realization,"[8] God reaches the realization of the self-created. God becomes God through incarnation in the Eternal Return; Aryan becomes Aryan through fighting for divine righteousness in the Cosmic Struggle.

2.

Already in 1926, Ernst Jünger saw the appearance of the Hitlerian State, kindred as he was to the Hitlerian Idea: "The shape of the future state has been made clear... It will be *national*. It will be *social*. It will be *armed*. Its structure will be *authoritarian*.... Such is the state of the future."[9] Jünger no doubt saw the exoteric aspects (*armed, authoritarian*) of the Hitlerian Reich because of his nation's sociopolitical situation; however, he also guessed these aspects must be integral to elevating the folk from their Weimarian quagmire. That is, in order for a folk who had been spiritually led astray — who had forgotten its Aryan roots — to be reoriented to its origins, order and discipline would have to be restored. Once restored, the exoteric trappings would fall aside.[10] Hitler himself had deftly explained *nationalism* and *socialism* to George Viereck in 1923:

> *Socialism* is the science of dealing with the common weal. Communism is not socialism. Marxism is not socialism. Marxists have stolen the term and confused its meaning. I shall take *socialism* away from the Socialists. *Socialism* is an ancient Aryan, Germanic institution. Our German ancestors held certain lands in common. They cultivated the idea of the common weal. Marxism has no right to disguise itself as socialism. *Socialism*, unlike Marxism, does not repudiate private property. Unlike Marxism, it involves *no negation of personality*, and unlike Marxism, it is *patriotic*.[11]

The Hitlerian State, then, was the means to restore the "ancient Aryan, Germanic institution" of socialism to the folk. This restoration would be the first step in the folk's reconciliation with God. Reconciliation with God is reached through an absolute duty to the Idea — to God and folk. Hitler's mention of *personality* and *patriotism* attests to this. *Personality* is the exhibition of one's character, of one's individual expression of God — that is, of one's will and the honoring of one's hereditary line; *patriotism* bears the same significance as *personality*: a patriot has *faith* in that which is *patrios* (*of one's fathers*). The restoration of God was a reclamation of value. Hitler elaborated on the criteria of value:

> People should be measured firstly by the work which they perform for their nation and secondly by their general character. It is not shouting *hurrah* but the willingness to subordinate their personal interest to those of the community, to those of the state, to subordinate their ego to the interest of all others which demonstrate their character.[12]

The National Socialist State's purpose was to reestablish the *character* of the Aryan race, to reorient the folk on themselves and, thus, God. The State was a political vessel with a spiritual purpose. To achieve this end, the Hitlerian State set capability,[13] good character, and a will-to-sacrifice as the criteria of value; these remain paramount among remaining Aryans to this day because these are the timeless criteria of the heroic type; these, too, are the same qualities embodied in the transformative God embarking on the salvific mission in the Eternal Return.

3.

Rudolf Hess left his family and fatherland to secure peace for a war in which he played little part beyond speechifying. For this, the Jews and their puppets imprisoned him for nearly five decades, after which they murdered him. They dared not release him — because to release him risked the revelation of the vile plan executed by their viler nature. But Hess was not the Spandau prisoner: *It is, instead, the jailers who are chained to the fatal fulfillment of the Myth* — so says Serrano.[14] Likewise, Hess, demonstrating the Aryan sacrifice, was prisoner of the Myth, destined to "fight a glorious desperate war."[15] *Myth* is the fate of the fighter in the Cosmic Struggle of the Eternal Return. Even the Jew fulfills its fate in the desperate war.

Hersch Lauterpacht, a Jew and principal force behind the concocted UN "war crimes" and subsequent Nuremberg Trials, all but created the legal framework to punish enemies of the Jewish World Order — *for all time*. Lauterpacht wrote the following indictment in 1944, in eager anticipation of condemning Jewry's enemies before the world; it was "eventually incorporated into the [International Military Tribunal's] judgment"[16]:

> The rules of warfare, like any other rules of international law, are binding not only upon impersonal entities, but upon human beings. The rules of law are binding not upon an abstract notion of Germany, but upon members of the German government, upon German individuals exercising governmental functions in occupied territory, upon German officers, upon German soldiers.[17]

"International law" is a legal construct meant (1) to safeguard Jews in their internationalist ambitions and (2) to provide sufficient power to prosecute parties hostile to Judeo-imperialism. The juristic framework above ensures the penalty trickles down to even the lowest-ranking soldier — *a true revelation of Jewish vengeance*. To this day, of course, we see nonagenarians humiliatingly wheeled before courts and broadcast across the globe for their role in this or that "international crime." These trials are nothing more than consequence-laden spectacles to mete out Jewish hatred and remind the Gentiles of what happens to those who resist Jewish Imperium. Any leader or nation who does not adhere to the Judeo-system has been, is, and will be punished (ultimately to death) for interference with the Jewish plan of sociopolitical domination. This legal framework was the basis for the *ad hoc* tribunal created to protect laws that were initially *invented* for the purpose of the proceedings, and was meant to give the whole charade an air of legitimacy, an air of the honorable execution of *abiding justice*. Robert Jackson, Chief Prosecutor for the United States, summarized the oft-perceived strengths of the Trial:

> That four great nations, flushed with victory and stung with injury stay the hand of vengeance and voluntarily submit their captive enemies to the judgment of the law is one of the most significant tributes that Power has ever paid to Reason.[18]

The Judeo-Allies were and are quite proud of their show-trial. That the defendants were not summarily executed is a badge of honor for a Jewish vengeance that would have no doubt wished to torture and maim both the defendants *and* their families. Instead of murdering them outright, the Judeo-Allies chose to execute only half the defendants and extend the suffering of the others for decades, if not a lifetime — *a true revelation of Jewish vengeance*.

There was no historical precedent for such trials, for such laws. Paul Rassinier, himself a former detainee in a German work-camp, argues against the idea of enforcing laws arbitrarily or retroactively, as was so clearly done in the postwar world:

> The non-retroactivity of laws is, in fact, one of the sacred principles of our culture. And if our moral system

holds that "ignorance of the law is not excusable," it is also claimed that where no law exists there can be no offence and consequently no punishment. *Nulla poena sine lege* ... [— this] remains the individual's only, and very harrow, protection against arbitrary power.¹⁹

Yet when we have laws so arbitrarily created *post hoc*, they can *only* be seen as punishment and the wielding of arbitrary power. Thus, what we see with the war trials (at Nuremberg and elsewhere) is not execution of abiding justice, but victors' vengeance; it is punishment, the so-called victors' justice — which is to say, not "justice" at all. The reality of such vengeance belies its true heritage; it certainly is not pre-Christian Roman, whose Latin is cited above: It is the Jewish channeling of Satan-Jehovah's wrath.

To confirm this, one need only to look at the very rules for the Tribunal, whose statutory presidents are the war's victors (Britain, France, the United States, and the Soviet Union):

> **Article 1** sets the conditions: *There shall be established an International Military Tribunal for the just and prompt trial and punishment of the major war criminals of the European Axis.*
>
> – The first article pronounces the Tribunal "just" and declares that the tried are "criminals" to be "punished."
>
> **Article 3** describes the desired justice: *Neither the Tribunal, its members nor their alternates can be challenged by the prosecution, or by the Defendants or their Counsel.*
>
> – The judges cannot be judged; victors set the rules. Of course, the members of the Tribunal cannot be challenged because to do so would reveal their own guilt in the arbitrarily, retroactively created laws.

Article 6 defines the nature of the crimes:
Crimes Against Peace: namely, planning, preparation, initiation or waging of a war of aggression, or a war in violation of international treaties, agreements or assurances, or participation in a common plan or conspiracy for the accomplishment of any of the foregoing.
- The Judeo-Allies began their provocations for a war against the Hitlerian State with the economic boycott of all German goods immediately following Hitler's winning the chancellorship. This rejection of a country's right to self-determination is diametrically opposed to the same plea for self-determination in the Axis constitutions drafted by the Judeo-Allies following the war.

War Crimes: namely, violations of the laws or customs of war. Such violations shall include, but not be limited to, murder, ill-treatment or deportation to slave labor or for any other purpose of civilian population of or in occupied territory, murder or ill-treatment of prisoners of war or persons on the seas, killing of hostages, plunder of public or private property, wanton destruction of cities, towns or villages, or devastation not justified by military necessity.
- Each of the member-states of the Tribunal, who could not be challenged (Article 3), committed war crimes — e.g., "strategic bombing," mass murder of German POWs, mass murder of German civilians, abuse of illiberal Germans, etc. All such criminality was mere destruction of German men, women, and children, melting like candles in a furnace of "justice."

Crimes Against Humanity: namely, murder, extermination, enslavement, deportation, and other inhumane acts committed against any civilian population, before or during the war; or persecutions on political, racial or religious grounds in execution of or in connection with any crime within the jurisdiction of the Tribunal, whether or not in violation of the domestic law of the country where perpetrated.

- There is no mention of possible crimes *after* the war; thus, the Judeo-Allies were free to "deprogram" the Axis nations any way they saw fit. Note again Britain and America's indiscriminate firebombing of countless German towns — designed and delivered for the sole purpose of "destroying the morale of the German people" and, consequently, their will to fight. Note the postwar "internment" camps the Allies established to punish regular German citizens. Note the blockades against the Germans (to include those after the war) designed and delivered to commit mass starvation. Note the Soviet Union's wanton destruction and pillaging of all things German during and after the war — and never forget the *unspeakable* atrocities the Soviets committed against German women and children.[20] Note the nuclear weapons dropped on Japanese citizens. And, lest we forget, the member states of the Tribunal cannot be challenged.

Article 9 states that the Tribunal may declare any group associated with the "war criminals" a "criminal organization." In this way, many uplifting, wholesome, and beautiful organizations in Hitler's Germany were thereby rendered "criminal." This is victors' justice *par excellence*. It is further stipulated in Article 9 that the Tribunal can decide what does and does not get heard before the court. This is undoubtedly related to Article 3, whereby the member-states cannot be challenged.

Article 10 notes that any organization recognized as "criminal" by the Tribunal can no longer be questioned as otherwise. This is not justice; this is *diktat*.

Article 11 states that if one is a recognized as a criminal, then one will be punished as a criminal.

Article 18 gives the Tribunal (i.e., the Tribunal gives itself) power to "rule out irrelevant issues and statements of any kind" — thus, any issues and statements counter to the Tribunal's aims of staying above the law it metes and punishing the defendants will be judged *irrelevant*.

Article 19: *The Tribunal shall not be bound by technical rules of evidence.*
- Alleged witness testimony, for instance, did not require forensic confirmation. Nearly anything — *rumor, hearsay, opinion* — could be accepted as *true* if it fit the Tribunal's predetermined verdict.

Article 20: *The Tribunal may require to be informed of the nature of any evidence before it is entered so that it may rule upon the relevance thereof.*

Article 21: *The Tribunal shall not require proof of facts of common knowledge...*
- The Tribunal considered the facts it deemed *relevant* "facts of common knowledge."

Article 26 gives the defendants no recourse to actual justice after the trial: *The judgment of the Tribunal as to the guilt or the innocence of any Defendant ... shall be final and not subject to review.*
- In other words, once a *war criminal*, always a *war criminal*.

Article 27 offers more godlike power to the member states: *The Tribunal shall have the right to impose upon a Defendant, on conviction, death or such other punishment as shall be determined by it to be just.*

Few people have ever looked at the articles undergirding the juristic vengeance that flowed from the Judeo-violence characterizing the war. The above articles are stressed to illustrate the hateful nature of the Judeo-system, which has increasingly governed all societies (particularly in the West) — from courtrooms to classrooms and boardrooms to bedrooms — since 1945. We are dominated by the Jewish impetus, the Jewish Imperium. The Jews' will is meant to become *ours*. And if we adopt the alien, we, in turn, lose our own identity — *for all time*. This is propaganda raised to a fever pitch in a Nuremberg that looks *utterly alien* — the harbinger of the alien world to follow, the debasement of man that turns familiar tradition into elusive memory. Meanwhile, most will keep using all the dispiriting, corrupting distractions of the Aryans' enemies: enter media and Hollywood, enter fast food and pharmaceuticals, enter indoctrinatory distortions and all things that undermine mental, physical, and spiritual health.

None of this is a crime, of course, because *Ahasuerus has the ear of the kings*; he has the money and "power" in this darkest of ages. And with his money and power Ahasuerus and his comrades scheme to destroy Aryan lifeways and, thus, Aryan destiny, by poisoning mind, body, and spirit. Such is the cost of combat in the Kali-Yuga, that darkest night before the distant, heroic dawn.

Carry the light of Aryan divinity into Satan-Jehovah's serpentine shadows and you act as a vessel for the looming Fury. Make yourself and your loved ones mentally, physically, and spiritually fit and you take the most anti-establishment, *anti-Jewish* position you can: through your very being you rail against a Judeo-system designed to keep you weak and docile, readymade for slavery to the Eternal Enemy. Carry the light and fight — for the *God who was* and the *God who is*.

Hitlerism promises nothing but reconciliation with God. All else is meaningless. If one is in harmony with the primordial spirit animating action, then one is that much closer to the Nature that deserves our reverence. Aryan spirit is honor and loyalty; it is God and family; it is conscientious sacrifice for the transcendent Cause of Causes.

The divinity of internal harmony can only attain external expression when disharmony is excised. The Judeo-system is disharmony. The Aryan is the implicit middle between God and Demiurge. Harmony and discord confront the Aryan: Your attentive choice defines your will.

Revelations: A Preface — Notes

[1] Martin Friedrich, *Hitler Avatāra* (2023), 48.
[2] Friedrich, *Hitler Avatāra*, 55.
[3] 01 May 1923 (speech).
[4] Søren Kierkegaard, *Purity of Heart is to Will One Thing* (1956), 54, 63: "The Good without condition and without qualification, without preface and without compromise is, absolutely the only thing that a man may and should will, and is only one thing.... Salvation lies only in the purity with which a man wills the Good." Cf. *Hitler Avatāra*.
[5] Kierkegaard, *Purity of Heart*, 59-60.
[6] Kierkegaard, *Purity of Heart*, 210.
[7] Miguel Serrano, *Resurrection of the Hero* (2015), 126.
[8] A.C.B. Swami Prabhupada, *Bhagavad-gītā As It Is* (1972), 75.
[9] Ernst Jünger, "Unite!" *Die Standarte* (June 1926).
[10] Even after Hitler became Führer of the Germanic folk, he and all his immediate subordinates knew there would not be another Führer: the very idea was *impossible*. There is only one Führer in the same way there is only one Avatāra. God does not bequeath incarnations.
[11] Originally published in *The American Monthly* (January 1923); reprinted as "When I take charge: Hitler shows his hand," *Liberty* (6 July 1932), p. 4. Cf. Hitler's 28 July 1922 speech: "Socialism in itself is *anything but* an international creation. As a noble conception it has indeed grown up exclusively in Aryan hearts: it owes its intellectual glories only to Aryan brains. *It is entirely alien to the Jew*."
[12] Adolf Hitler, 18 January 1927 (speech).
[13] "We should judge people according to the abilities with which nature has endowed them and which they use for the benefit of the community." Adolf Hitler, 18 January 1927 (speech). Equal opportunity for viable kinsmen was the other aspect of the capability criterion.
[14] Miguel Serrano, *Adolf Hitler: The Ultimate Avatar* (2014), 61.
[15] Serrano, *Adolf Hitler*, 324.
[16] *The International Court of Justice: custodian of the archives of the International Military Tribunal at Nuremberg* (Nuremberg Trial Archives, 2018), 27. Hereafter cited as *International Court of Justice*.
[17] Lauterpacht, *British Year Book of International Law* (1944), "The Law of Nations and Punishment of War Crimes."
[18] *International Court of Justice*, 15-16.
[19] Paul Rassinier, *The Real Eichmann Trial* (2002), 30.
[20] The researchers and translators at *Donauschwaben Villages Helping Hands* have done fine work recording Soviet atrocities against the Germanic people (www.dvhh.org). Their work captures only some of

the countless genocidal actions perpetrated in postwar Europe. See also Bacque's *Other Losses*, Keeling's *Gruesome Harvest*, Goodrich's *Hellstorm: The Death of Nazi Germany 1944-1947*, Bradberry's *The Myth of German Villainy*, among others. John Sack, a Jew himself, reflected on postwar Europe: "the Jews ... killed a great number of Germans: ... German men, women, children, *babies*, whose 'crime' was just to be Germans" (*Eye for an Eye* [1993], x).

— 1 —
Accelerationism and the Judeo-System

> *We are the Sons and Daughters of Shiva. Our purpose is the restoration of God and Nature. In this time of evil urges — in the time of the Demiurge — we focus our efforts on accelerating the coming collapse. We prepare for the coming of Kalki and Shiva; what follows in their wake is beyond us.*
>
> — *Hitler Avatāra*

1.

Hitlerist accelerationism is the idea that society, in this Jewish Age, is *irredeemably* wicked and must be disintegrated. What waits on the other side of this disintegration is neither known nor sought in and of itself. Hitlerist accelerationism recognizes only the cosmic unrighteousness of a Jewish World Order and seeks its destruction *for all time*. "In the face of radical evil," thought Carl Schmitt, "the only solution is dictatorship"[1] — Hitlerism is the dictatorship of cosmic righteousness.[2]

A post-collapse "utopia" is practicable only after Providence deems it so; still, however, no such "utopia" is the goal of Hitlerist accelerationism. Man's wickedness — molded and guided by relentless Judeo-materialism — is malignant and infects every aspect of this world, animate and inanimate, so that we are left with three types of being:

1. The Rulers: Jews and their accomplices;
2. The Ruled: the dreck, masses of *nihilists*;
3. The Rebels: dissenters who recognize Nature's supremacy.

Much has been said about the Jews and their helpers; and although many exceptional thinkers have written on the subject, one need look no further than *Mein Kampf*, for no other work is as incisive or carries such immediacy. Adolf Hitler was right about the Jews; hardly anything further needs to be said on the matter. Though, for curiosity's sake, a onetime, self-proclaimed professional intimate recalled Hitler disclosing this judgment:

> Two worlds face one another — the men of God and the men of Satan! The Jew is the anti-man, the creature of another god. He must have come from another root of the human race. I set the Aryan and the Jew over against each other; and if I call one of them a human being I must call the other something else. The two are as widely separated as man and beast. Not that I would call the Jew a beast. He is much further from the beasts than we Aryans. He is a creature outside Nature and alien to Nature.[3]

Apocryphal or not, the above powerfully captures the sentiment Hitler often laid bare: "the Jewish people in itself stands against us [Aryans] as our deadly foe and so will stand against us always and *for all time*."[4] Hitler said this in 1922, before even the *putsch* that landed him in the Landsberg prison where he would write *Mein Kampf*; revealing the Jew was his program from the beginning. Fundamentally, Jews are the bearers of a system that is the material basis of their essence; Jews impose this Judeo-system for their benefit at the expense of non-Jews; such is the eternal, parasitical nature of the Jew.

Next, the ruled — the unwitting masses — are *nihilistic* simply because they are ignorant of the Cosmic Struggle; barring happy accidents, none of their actions carry the weighty mindfulness necessary to combat the godless, anti-Nature urges of the Enemy; in short, if they do not conscientiously take a side in the Struggle, their actions not only lack moral import, they also stand as a *rebellion against meaning*. "It is necessary to take a conscious *one-sided position*," instructs Jünger. "The time has come to *put an end to* the senseless ambition for *objectivity* which only leads to *relativism* and doubt in one's own strength."[5] An attack against meaning is Nihilism. Some might see in the meaningless majority a latent power in need only of "convincing"[6]; some might see them as an enemy; their side has been chosen by *not* consciously choosing a side, however, and they can only be enemies of righteousness. Still, the end marches nearer. Finally are the rebels, or those dissenters who recognize Nature's supremacy: these hardy souls needn't be Hitlerists — few are. Rebels reject the status quo of the Judeo-system, regardless of their interpretation of it, and seek its demise — *because it is the most righteous act*. Thus, rebels subscribe to proper accelerationism.

While the so-called "right" and oblivious system-supporters bicker about what is and is not *accelerationism*, while "traditionalists" vehemently divide themselves along philosophic-semantic lines, the end draws nearer nonetheless. It is typical of the "right" that they should be caught unawares — that the world should pass them by while they decide what book to read or what contemptuous comment to make about their supposed kinsmen. The modern "right" isn't real; it is hardly more than an experiment, a pacifying foray into the ideological night, a puppet whose strings are manipulated by unrighteous impulses. When the "traditionalist" matures, he will consider putting on his socks[7] — he will move the money from his mattress to his 401(k).

What *is* real is our unabating march toward societal decay, and this is all the better. This march cannot be stopped; if it cannot be stopped, its hastening is *immaterial*. However, if Hitlerism is the pursuit of cosmic righteousness, *any* fight against the cosmic unrighteousness that is the Jewish World Order will naturally entail a struggle that works toward the fall of this system. If society elevates the farcical "We the People" — the *quantity* — to the heavens, the Hitlerist fights for the grounding truth of unequivocal character — the *quality*; if miscegenation is foisted upon the unwitting herd, the Hitlerist holds all the more firmly to his kinfolk; if mass ignorance through media-entertainment-technological distractions is encouraged, the Hitlerist hardens himself through experiential living; if society works to indoctrinate each new generation through depraved educational systems, the Hitlerist seeks to instruct himself through edifying study; if society aims to eradicate God-Nature-family, then the Hitlerist deems these life-givers *dearer than life itself*. To the point of self-sacrifice does the Hitlerist act in his fight against cosmic unrighteousness. This is not "political" misstep, as some have argued[8]; this is divine duty, it is the *absolute* duty to God that faith demands. *Even if the world came to an end, the commandment must nonetheless be carried out when the call is heard.*[9]

The "political" victory imagined by "ethnocentrists" is impossible because it is naught but faithless materialism — as if all that is needed is to *convince* just *one more white* of the "metapolitical" cause. The *convincing* stage — just like the political stage — *is over*. Instead, what the present situation demands, Kaczynski held,

> is not ... to persuade the majority of people that we're right, so much as to try to increase tensions in society to the point where things start to break down, when people get uncomfortable enough so that they're going to rebel. Now the question is, how do you increase those tensions?[10]

Tensions have been elevated and civilizations destabilized since the Jews parasitized their first society; and methods to exacerbate tensions and subvert prevailing systems have changed little in several hundred generations. The task now — the *difference* now — is to conduct such activity in defense of God and Nature, which necessarily works against the Jew and its Judeo-system. Attempts at persuasion presume there are intelligent and honorable minds ready to listen; generally, there are not. A great many people are *Lebensunwertes Leben*, or *lives unworthy of life*. Moreover, if one is not convinced of pervading socio-spiritual unrighteousness now, *one never will be*. Savitri Devi tells us:

> One does not *become* a National Socialist. One only discovers, sooner or later, that one has always been one — that, by nature, one could not possibly be anything else. For this is not a mere political label; not an "opinion" that one can accept or dismiss according to circumstances, but a faith, involving one's whole being,

physical and psychological, mental and spiritual: "not a new election cry, but a new conception of the world" — a way of life — as our Führer himself has said."

What many "ethnocentrists" neglect is that race is not only a biological concept, but also a spiritual one. When the Jew Leon Trotsky says, "the Soviet Union is an immense *melting pot* in which the characters of dozens of nationalities are being mixed" and "the mysticism of the 'Slavic soul' is coming off like *scum*," we are granted an insight into the Judeo-mind.[12] From this revelation we learn that (1) the notion of the *melting pot* is shared across internationalist ideologies — e.g., America has proudly been a "melting pot"[13] for decades; (2) the Judeo-Marxist believes eradicating biological race is essential to its aims; (3) the Judeo-Marxist believes eradicating spiritual race is essential to its aims; (4) the mystic (i.e., spiritual-cultural) soul is "scum." Even the Jew acknowledges the spiritual aspect of the racial soul! Of course, this is well known; otherwise, the Jew would not have survived for millennia in tact, nor would the Jew have obsessed over "open societies" and "equality" in its host communities since its ascent in Europe centuries ago.

While not equivalent, *race* and *soul* are nevertheless inextricably linked: if one "melts ... off like scum," the other, too, will disappear; the result will be a biologically and spiritually blank mass ready for molding. Hitlerism rejects the Yockeyite position that races are fluid in any jarring, supra-material sense:

> We are not unfamiliar with the man who, after associating with Jews ... becomes a Jew in the fullest sense of the word.... The converse is also known: many Jews have adopted Western feelings and rhythms, and have thereby acquired Western race.[14]

The *purely spiritual* notion of race, like the *purely material* notion, is fantasy. Yockey decried the Hitlerist conception of race as a product of "19th century materialism." However, the Hitlerist conception acknowledges both the material *and* spiritual aspects of race — not one or the other alone. Yockey, on the other hand, posits only a *spiritual* concept of race, but has an utterly *materialistic* concept of reality (i.e., he does not recognize the Cosmic Struggle). *The recognition of both material and spiritual realities is central to Hitlerism.* As Hitler himself wrote,

> Once a people no longer appreciates the *cultural expression of its own spiritual life conditioned through its blood*, or even begins to feel ashamed of it and thereby turns its attention to alien expressions of life, it renounces the strength which lies in the harmony of its blood and the cultural life which has sprung from it.[15]

With this understanding, the Jew can never, as Yockey states, "acquire Western race" — this is impossible. Though it dedicates a life of service to the Aryan cause, a Jew will forever be a Jew and must answer to its god. Contrary to this, if an Aryan abandons his blood in service to the Judeo-system, this Aryan is lost forever to the spiritual-cultural identity of his former folk. This is the Hitlerist view of race.

Because of this connection between race and soul, *faith* must play a major — if not *central* — role in any cause to restore righteousness.[16] Persuasion, then, plays only a peripheral role on the path to Hitlerism; proofs can only serve to make one attentive to the individual decision of faith, but no one is ever *convinced* of this or that ideology: one's spiritual-cultural soul simply resonates with a particular ideology or it does not. Thus, one does not *become* a Hitlerist; one simply is or is not.

Hitlerists are often seen as anachronistic, as "stubbornly grasping at the past" or living "off the capital of the past instead of feeding off the energies of the present" and are thus "doomed to futility"[17]; on the contrary: Hitlerists believe only the first step toward solution has been realized: the unmasking of the Eternal Enemy; the next step has not yet come — for *the Reich that will come is no longer of this world, nor of this sun*.[18] Politicking as the "next step," rather, is living in the past and doomed. Accelerationism, on the other hand, is the nebulous *ceasing of all steps* — nebulous because it has *never been tried*; it is the embrace of a present whose character has been decided by a future that has already happened.

Political victory is materially impossible because it presumes a unified familial and societal state. Political victory was within reach in Hitler's Germany because a meaningful cultural-spiritual homogeneity still existed; no such uniformity exists in the West, however. Western "traditionalists" — those who want to conserve cultural-spiritual values — are born of every stripe and march under every banner. They are united only in their bungling pigheadedness. Here are Christians, there are atheists; here are hardline racialists, there are culturalists; we have National Socialists and Fascists; Hitlerists and Yockeyites; materialists and spiritualists; dualists and monists; political-solutionists and accelerationists — in short, we hear a clamor masking the constant encroachment of those who aim to destroy us.

But — and this is significant — there *is no* "us." The red-bearded, blue-eyed, barrel-chested "freedom" fighter and face-tattooed jackbooter yelling *Sieg Heil!* in the public square have no more in common with the supposed esotericist seeking "ancient Hyperborea" than does the Aryan with the Jew. Should we acknowledge their white skin? What is "whiteness" when one is spiritually bankrupt? One may as well be a Marxist or even a world-destroying Jew! Is the random "white" man one sees on the street a "brother" because he shares a European ancestry? What does the dead look in his eyes reveal? What of his slouched shoulders and flabby body? What of the parade of pills he pours down his throat? And how about the diversity-pushing and money-loving "white" corporate executive? Is he or she a kinsman?

Race is the beginning of everything, but it is not everything. No "white" man is ever a kinsman unless he lives honorably — i.e., unless he seeks mental, physical, and spiritual fitness, unless he *comprehends* faith. No one is good simply because of *melanin* counts, and any ideology spouting "white brotherhood" or "white people" or "ethnocentrism" is nothing more than a preposterous materialism on par with Judeo-Marxism. Yes, win your *political* victories with your "metapolitical" narratives, perhaps even your "jackbooting"; you can exchange pats on the back with your Jewish comrades in the halls of Congress.

Hitlerism seeks no political end — *Götterdämmerung* was the *end* of a political solution. While such a solution was "within reach" for the Third Reich, it was yet impossible — *impossible* because it did not occur.

> A real revolution has not happened yet, but its marching step can already be heard! This is not a reaction, but an authentic revolution with all its telltale signs and slogans, its idea is the *völkisch*, sharpened to an unprecedented edge, its banner — the swastika, its political expression — the concentration of *will*, a dictatorship! It will replace word with *deed*, ink with *blood*, empty phrases with *sacrifices*, the pen with the *sword*.[19]

These are lofty words from Ernst Jünger and, coming in 1923, quite prescient. The dictatorship Jünger yearned for here certainly did come to pass, but, as we know, it did not last. *It could not last.* Speak of accidental properties all you like; it does not change the reality of the situation: Hitler's Reich ended and *Götterdämmerung* was the rise of the Jew. *It could have been otherwise* is the coward's call. *It could have been otherwise* is the plaintive pleading of the material-minded. "Within reach" is a fantasy — rather, it is the catalyst that might serve to make us attentive.[20] We should be attentive to the real aim of Adolf Hitler's life and mission: *to expose the Jew — the Eternal Enemy — for all time.* Yes, *Götterdämmerung* was the rise of the Jew, but it was also the rise of the Hitlerist — that bold creature who defies *insurmountable odds* set against him by a world that stands as the defender of its own demise.

Adolf Hitler, among other things, was a political figure; but his *goal* was not political — he was no "ethnocentrist." To be sure, Hitler was the Hero of *Europe*, the Savior of *European* Culture, and as such would have worked for *European* welfare — but to save a "white" man simply because of his race? That blasphemy was beneath him.[21] More "Aryans" than Jews died before, during, and after the war, both in camps and out of them — i.e., more people of Germanic descent, more "whites." The vacant-eyed, self-medicated "Aryan"; the wild-eyed, fluorescent-haired "Aryan"; the average, overweight, fantasy-fetishizing "Aryan" who lives vicariously through sports; the "Aryan" whose face looks like an abortion of almighty science — *their outward appearance is a reflection of their soul*, and each belongs with the rest of the dreck — in a camp or out. Perhaps there is a place for them in the ranks of the *Sieg Heil*-ing jackbooters causing a *political* ruckus and getting their faces tattooed; perhaps there is room for them among the Marxian rejects vying for some collectivist, guilt-ridden significance. "The nobody is always eager to imagine himself a somebody, [and] the man who is a misfit in his own society is always a liberal out of self-preservation."[22]

Certainly, those seeking *political* victory in the postwar world are essentially liberalists. And however they manifest, they do not belong in Hitler's ranks; they are no Hitlerists — *fodder*, perhaps, but not Hitlerists. Of the dregs who are at least politically aware, all are materialists reflecting a poisoned soul with their rancorous façade; dregs they remain, however, and dregs are naught but fodder for the Judeo-system. They are the slag left over from the smelted gold of the White Gods; in Serrano's words, they are

> the men of diminished stature who now inhabit the martyrized surface of the earth, [they] are the surviving slaves of Atlantis and Lemuria, the men-"robots," the men-ants, the animal-men who caused the cataclysm and who will bring about its repetition through their rebelliousness and their ignorant pride. They are the *Elementaruresen* against whom the *Wildes Heer* ... will fight their final battle.[23]

And in this battle, all will be consumed by fire — the fire of Vesuvius, on whose slopes are built the Hitlerist encampments.

Before he became jaded by those practical "ethnocentrists" who sought to turn the spiritual into the material, and by his own descent into politico-materialism, Ernst Jünger was an idealist and perhaps the most faithful inheritor of Nietzsche's legacy[24]:

> We do not wish to hear of chemical reactions, blood injections, skull shapes and Aryan profile. All this sooner or later will result in ugliness and petty squabbles that open the door for the intellect into the world of values that it is incapable of comprehending and can only destroy.[25]

"[Hitlerism is not] for everyone. It is for the heroes who still *aspire to divinity*, to *immortality*."[26] The Hitlerist is a man or woman of *faith* — faith in the *event* and *advent* of Adolf Hitler, faith in God, faith in family, faith in the downfall of both the Judeo-system and the insurmountable odds stacked against the righteous. Anything that is *not* faith is merely means to an end and never an end in itself. As Hitler said: "The greatest task of all will be to make it as clear as possible ... that *this Party is not an end in itself*, but merely a *means to an end*."[27] The Party — i.e., the *political* — was, *exclusively* in this time so ideologically distant, the means to the end that was cosmic righteousness — i.e., a restoration of honor, loyalty, and decency — which is to say, *piety*.[28]

The Hitlerist solution is not a political one; politics are no longer viable in a Judeo-system that has long directed the levers of material existence. Rather, the Hitlerist solution is *dissolution*; it is *acceleration* — acceleration of the end that will come *with* or *without* him. It is the Hitlerist's duty to fight for righteousness, to fight for God; this duty defines him; this duty is his *hope* and man's *salvation*. When creative men who reflect their Creator God can only serve with their creativity a Judeo-system that seeks their demise, then their creativity must turn to ends perceived as inimical by that very system, i.e., their creativity must turn to destruction. *Winning by losing* is not "losing by losing," as the materialistic "ethnocentrists" say; it is, in fact, *winning*: When the Judeo-system, which precludes victory from inside its construct, falls, the righteous work will have been completed.

How can one speak of *losing* when the most divine end is achieved? Only a brash materialist can think in such a way: *Don't take life from me — I'll compromise with whomever is necessary — just leave me my politics!* It turns out those so concerned with *winning-by-winning*²⁹ are hardly more than posers. The materialistic strategy of *winning-by-winning* brings only materialistic ends; defeat, on the other hand, leads, as Jünger reminds us, to the

> [concentration of] all inner strength and [the establishment of] a solid foundation for the future.... Defeat [teaches] us to confirm our faith with blood, it [restores] our connection with the soil, it ... [gives] depth to feelings.³⁰

Geist emanating from blood: one must have it to begin to understand the leap.

Hitlerists would rather "live in a world full of *meaning* than to drown in a characterless gruel..."³¹ — even if that meaning expires with the martyr on the individual level. And note: accelerationism is no morbid suicide mission; it is the *awareness* of a moribund world metastasized with Judeo-materialism and the *fervent desire* to stop it. If efforts to restore the righteousness revealed in the advent of Hitler Avatāra culminate in personal sacrifice, then all the better: "We shall be willing to sacrifice and fight, and would rather pass away ourselves than allow that [restoration of righteousness] to pass away which is [our] last strength, last hope, and last future."³²

What is this future? It is the path of pious partisans who live as if the Jew has been unmasked *for all time*; it is the burgeoning of meaning in the souls of the living sparked by the sacrifice of the martyred. The Hitlerist fights his war *without conditions*, for it is a war against the evilest Enemy and for the resurrection of the greatest Good; and *a war unleashed without conditions will always be a war won. Even when lost.*³³ "Adolf Hitler, when the end approached, remained immovable with ever-greater *fanaticism*. The greatest fires forge his iron will, his Teutonic fury, transforming his blood into fire."³⁴ *Immovability* is not compromise; *fanaticism* is not politics; and winning through politics or persuasion is not a solution.

What follows in the collapse's wake is *beyond us* — it is for the materialists to ponder. If, by some miracle, honorable folk remain after the collapse, they will perhaps create something good — something good that will inevitably be corrupted, because the *good* men who follow the *strong* men of hard times carry too much *sun* and not enough *lightning*.[35] Collapse is certain, as our Aryan ancestors foretold: whether it happens in the next month or in another 425,000 years is uncertain. Ours is not to reason *when*, ours is but to accelerate the end.[36]

This does not mean the Hitlerist cause is *nihilistic* — far from it. In 1997, the Earth Liberation Front declared itself the "burning rage of a dying planet … to speed up the collapse of industry, to scare the rich, and to undermine the foundations of the state."[37] Similarly, Hitlerists are this "burning rage of a dying planet," which echoes a primal divinity and makes our soul sing, and such a "burning rage" can only be considered *nihilistic* from the perspective of the Judeo-system itself.[38] Actions and ends pregnant with *meaning* are never nihilistic, as Nihilism is only that which *spurns* meaning. What more meaning could exist than the fanatical support of one idea and the fanatical rejection of another? Our efforts *pregnant with meaning* fill us with the euphoria of a genuine holy communion: "When hot blood rushes through our veins, we get an inkling of what great forces all living things possess. Only having restored a connection with the Earth will we be able to feel communion with all things," as a more enlivened Jünger wrote.[39] Joseph Goebbels, too, noted the spiritual-communal character of revolutionary Hitlerism:

> Revolutions are *spiritual* acts. They appear first in people, then in politics and the economy. New people form new structures. The transformation we want is first of all *spiritual*; that will necessarily change the way things are.
>
> This revolutionary act is *beginning* to be visible in us. The result is a *new type of person* visible to the knowing eye: the National Socialist. Consistent with his *spiritual* attitude, the National Socialist makes *uncompromising* demands in politics. There is no *if* and *when* for him, only an *either/or*.[40]

National Socialism was the political form of the spiritual Hitlerist movement, which, at the time, was meant to enable Europe's transition from *a once-fearsome people under Germanic influence that had been lulled into docile complicity with a Judeo-system* to *a revitalized, spiritually charged folk capable of communing with the transcendent*. The revolutionary fanaticism at the core of National Socialism was the political means, in that time of greater cultural-spiritual homogeneity, to accomplish the transcendent end. Adolf Hitler himself insisted, "Those who see in National Socialism nothing more than a political movement know scarcely anything of it. It is more even than a religion: it is the will to create mankind anew."[41] We can say, with full sincerity and justification, that Hitlerism is the will to commune with the transcendent.

There are, of course, some that call Hitler's Reich *nihilistic* for revoking the Judeo-system yoking the whole world: they are called *Jews* — by spirit or blood. Jünger himself even began to see the Hitlerian Idea as *nihilistic* when, after the flagrant rise of the Jewish World Order in 1945, he commenced to more openly critique the *totalitarian* character Hitler's political experiment assumed; this latter point, however, only highlights the failings of politics-as-solution and reveals a late-Jüngerian shift to the *political*, which controverts his earlier focus on the passionate, world-changing *Idea* (i.e., the Hitlerian Idea).

Predating, and perhaps even foreshadowing, Jünger's descent into the political, Hermann Rauschning, an erstwhile and estranged NSDAP official, wrote some sensational accounts of his here-transcribed, there-fabricated conversations with Hitler. Rauschning, a traditional German liberal-conservative, was adamant that Hitler betrayed the liberal-conservative revolution and instead prescribed a *nihilistic* revolution:

> [The National Socialists] wanted [a] complete liberation from the past, on which to build a *totalitarian* despotism.... They see life's meaning in its perils, life's purpose as domination, the means as violence, and the goal as worldwide totalitarian empire.[42]

The interest in the Reich's *totalitarian* character is telling, for it is this feature, and not any *lack* of meaning, that marks the Reich as *nihilistic* for Rauschning and Jünger; the concern is *where* meaning is placed, and *not* that there is an absence of meaning. Of course, the "traditionalists" and their politics-as-solution mentality — in both Hitler's time and ours — are precisely part of the problem; it is only natural, then, that they would take affront at a revolutionary *Idea* meant to trample them *for all time*.[43] It cannot be overemphasized that *politics*, for Hitler, was only ever a means to an end — the end being *the revelation of the International Jew as the world's Eternal Enemy*. In the end, it seems *nihilist* is the epithet hurled at the *knight of faith* before the world burns.[44]

2.

"Faith," Kierkegaard tells us, "is namely this paradox that the single individual is higher than the [ethical] ... in such a way that the movement repeats itself, so that after having been in the [ethical] he as the single individual isolates himself as higher than the [ethical]."[45] One is born into or arises out of the ethical, which can be thought of as the general morality guiding a given society; as such, one is subsumed by — or subordinate to — the ethical.

However, when one is compelled to follow a divine imperative that puts him at odds with the ethical, one is placed in a relational position of paradoxical superiority over and against the ethical that defines his action; that is, the *individual* vaults above the ethical in an *absolute relation to God*,[46] wherein any action now becomes, in essence, amoral. *All that matters is the individual and his relationship to God*. (Nietzsche, too, captured this idea: "What is done out of love always takes place beyond good and evil."[47]) Thus, a divinely inspired act that might be considered immoral in the *ethical* sense is certainly not immoral in the *individual* sense, i.e., the *divine* sense. Faith, then, is *duty to God*; and if Kierkegaard's logic is followed to the end, it is a *duty to oneself*. This juxtaposition with the ethical alone, however, is insufficient to elevate one to a *knight of faith*. One must further believe in the attainment of that which is already lost.

When one is resigned to losing that which is dear, one makes the final movement before faith: this is the *infinite resignation*. The resignation is infinite because "in the finite world there is much that is not possible.... [Infinite resignation], however, makes this impossibility possible by expressing it spiritually, but [the man of faith] expresses it spiritually by renouncing it."[48] If we rightly imagine the *infinite resignation* as concurrent with any movement of faith,[49] we can simply say that it is *the assurance of things hoped for, the conviction of things not seen*. Thus, when one distinctly and simultaneously renounces God's assurance and yet, *against all odds*, rests assured of its eventuality, one becomes a *knight of faith*.

Now we see why the political-solutionists will never comprehend victory or defeat, Hitlerism or, indeed, reality: they lack an understanding of, if not the ability for, *faith*. Before he lost his sense of the Idea, Jünger understood things like *infinite resignation* and *paradoxicality*: "the spirit needs blood, for it is *life itself*, it doesn't need consciousness"[50] — those clinging to consciousness for consciousness' sake are naught but materialists, *nihilists* — an enemy in disguise.

3.

Daniel Byman, a Jewish researcher for the Brookings Institute, noted,

> accelerationism is an admission of weakness... Its proponents [recognize] that, on their own, they cannot foment the revolution they seek ... [nor] are they able to use the political system to achieve their ends, as leaders of the alt-right would endorse. Instead, they must latch on to existing societal problems and try to shape and exploit them.[51]

The Jew, like the "alt-right" or "ethnocentrists," sees using the political system to achieve its ends as a sign of strength; accelerationism, according to "them" collectively, on the other hand, "is an admission of weakness." It is worth emphasizing that this is but one point of agreement between the Jew and the so-called "alt-right" and "ethnocentrists." This agreement only represents both parties' affinity for moderation — *politics*, after all, is merely another name for *collective moderation*. We recall Hitler's loathing of moderation: "No! A thousand times No! There are only two possibilities: *either victory or defeat!*"⁵² Victory in *spirit* might very well mean a defeat in *politics*: men of character could hardly ask for more.

Is it an expression of weakness to want to destroy a Jewish means of control, a Jewish system of exploitation that will only itself end in destruction? Well, it certainly is an admission of a quantitative disadvantage; however, it is unlikely an espouser of any clear-headed accelerationism would characterize the *lack* of mechanical mobs as "weakness." Following the divine arc — *Providence* — is not weakness. It is *necessary* the world falls into disrepair, into degeneracy. It is *necessary* the disgusting quantity overshadows quality. It is all God's will in accordance with the amalgam of time. Fate is not weakness. *I will build a New Order from a New Man*, Hitler is recorded to have said. Anything more than this, however,

> he only intended to make public when he was no longer living. Then there would be … an *overwhelming revelation*. In order to completely fulfill his mission, he must die a martyr's death. "Yes," [Hitler said], "in the hour of supreme peril I must sacrifice myself for the people."⁵³

Giovanni Gentile advised the faithful to *recognize the advantage in sacrifice*:

> The mature men, the wise ones, smiled and calculated, and were horrified by the thought, as they would say, of *futile sacrifices*. They trembled at those dangers that, because of prudence, had never been confronted and would never be confronted by anyone not animated by an *indemonstrable faith*…. [Tepid] spiritual temperament is of the old style. It undertakes no effort because of a *lack of belief*; it flees from courage because *no advantage is recognized in the sacrifice*, measuring national fortunes only in terms of individual well-being, preferring always to travel where the way is solid, never to compromise oneself, never to become involved, leaving ideals to poets, to women, and particularly to philosophers, setting aside every question that

might jeopardize the settled and quiet life, and is content making jest of everything and anything, always seeking to deflate any poetic enthusiasm, recommending *moderation at all costs...*⁵⁴

The sacrifice is of one's personal ambitions, and perhaps even one's welfare, for the sake of the whole; but this precept extends beyond the individual and also applies to the group as a whole, for the group is the transcendent link to God. Individual action is only good and meaningful if it lends itself to the tribe.⁵⁵ Clausewitz's eternal words on our holy duty and the necessity of duty-despite-the-consequences speak directly to us:

> I believe and declare that a folk [must defend] the dignity and freedom of its existence ... to the last drop of blood. [I]t has no holier duty to fulfill, no higher law to obey. [T]he shame of a cowardly submission can never be erased ... [and] this drop of poison in the blood of a folk ... will corrupt and undermine the strength of future generations.... [A] folk bravely fighting for its freedom is invincible ... [and] even the loss of freedom after an honorable and bloody battle secures the rebirth of the folk and is the seed of life from which, one day, a new tree will strike firm root....⁵⁶

So what if — *what if* — the whole Germanic folk falls and spills its *last drop of blood*? What if all of Europe passes into docile enslavement or extinction? These are questions for the materialist — the "last men"⁵⁷ —, never the Hitlerist. Did we fight with everything we had for *righteousness* — for Nature, for God? If yes, we are righteous. God will sort out what comes of our efforts. Politicking is the Jews' game — especially since 1945; the Aryan fights — *to the last drop of blood*. Nature can take care of herself; but did we fight for her *nonetheless*?

What of the MAN TO COME?⁵⁸ Do we not also fight for him? Indeed. The MAN TO COME is but the whisper of God's approval in our soul. We fight for faith; we fight for God; we fight for Nature and her pitiless laws. We fight with absolute conviction in the God-commanded cause. This fight is beyond the universal ethical; this struggle is beyond good and evil. When we look to the future, we see *nothing* — but not in the *nihilistic* sense: we see *nothing to lose*. And for this we have everything to gain.

4.

Ernst Jünger's *On Pain* (1934) is valuable as both an historical and philosophical document, mainly because its moral philosophy reflected the end of the nationalistic (or what we today would call the "ethnocentric") age. We examine it here because, divorced from its now-defunct nationalistic outlook, the Nihilism of which Jünger speaks is all the more clear. The reader is encouraged to read it first as an historical document with nationalism in mind, then to reread it in the context of globalism — or the modern schema of technocratic corporatism — with a view to understanding its philosophical application.

> Today, we see the valleys and plains full of armies, military deployments, and exercises. We see states more hostile and ready for war than ever before, looking everywhere to expand their power and marshaling military forces and arsenals of weaponry, and their essential aim is no longer in doubt. We also see the individual ever more clearly fall into a state where he can be sacrificed without a second thought. The question thus arises whether we are witnessing the opening act of the spectacle to come, in which life appears as the will to power, and nothing else? ...
>
> [T]he only things beyond doubt are the destruction of old cults, the impotency of culture, and the wretched mediocrity of the actors.
>
> We ... find ourselves in a last and indeed quite remarkable phase of nihilism characterized by the broad expansion of new social orders with corresponding values yet to be seen. Once one has grasped the uniqueness of this situation, the seemingly contradictory view

of man disappears. One grasps how an enormous organizational capacity can exist alongside a complete blindness vis-à-vis values, belief without meaning, discipline without legitimacy — in short, the surrogate nature of ideas, institutions, and individuals altogether. One grasps why one yearns to see the state in such an instrumental age, not as the most universal instrument, but as a cultic entity, and why technology and ethos have become synonymous in such a peculiar way.

These are all indications that one has already completely pierced the side of the process rooted in obedience, training, and discipline; in short, the side of the human will. And never before have more advantageous circumstances existed for an incantation, superior to the purely moral will, to lend meaning to the not inappreciable virtue of ants. Man's relation to prophecy reveals that in his innermost being he is aware of the situation. For him, the *status quo* in all the states is just the basis for, or transition to, a future social order.

In such a situation, pain remains the only measure promising a certainty of insights. Wherever values can no longer hold their ground, the movement toward pain endures as an astonishing sign of the times; it betrays the negative mark of a metaphysical structure.

The practical consequence of this observation for the individual is, despite everything, the necessity to commit oneself to the preparation for war — regardless of whether he sees in it the preparatory stage of ruin or believes he sees on the hills covered with weather-worn crosses and wasted palaces the storm preceding the establishment of new orders of command.[59]

Jünger wrote about this "last phase" of Nihilism with "values yet to be seen" in 1934. Nearly a century later, these values are manifest; we need not record them here — look at Europe and her progeny: Is their blood ascending? Does honor exist in their heaths and hearths? Much has been paved under — from heaths to blood — and much that remains is numb to the world they reflect. Jünger begins his work with a quote from Inazo Notibé's *Bushido*; it is a mother scolding her child: "What a coward to cry for a trifling pain! What will you do when your arm is cut off in battle? What when you are called upon to commit *hara-kiri*?" What is the lesson? Jünger notes:

> Pain as a measure of man is unalterable, but what can be altered is the way he confronts it. Man's relation to pain changes with every significant shift in fundamental belief. This relation is in no way set; rather, it eludes our knowledge, and yet is the best benchmark by which to discern a race. We can observe this clearly today, since we have a novel and peculiar relation to pain in a world without binding norms....
>
> Our question is: What role does pain play in the new race we have called the *worker* that is now making its appearance on the historical stage?[60]

Man's ability to confront pain remains his litmus test even in this final phase of Nihilism. The result of this test, when all is paved under, is clear: It is not merely race that has gone under, but even "the worker" which has "replaced" it. We see the end approaching, but we are content with the status quo that mesmerizingly suggests a future of relative comfort. Yes, in this final stage of Nihilism the "values yet to be seen" are now visible; but the practical consequence of this observation is no longer the preparation for war, for the war is already lost. Instead, we face the consequence of a dumb docility. We have been lulled to sleep by our aversion to pain; we are the child scolded in *Bushido*; we perpetuate the war waged against us, and this, because it distances us from pain, makes us happy. It is almost beyond comprehension. What salvages the thought for our reason is the profound emptiness of man in this nihilistic age.

5.

Three men stand on a burial ground: a warrior, a priest, and a projection. They are together in space, but not in time: the warrior thrashes the past; the priest proselytizes the present; the projection lights the future.

Each one radiates a feeling peculiar to their time, but their connection with space is the same. The earth covers the dead; they are the living: the earth is objectified; they are elevated. Distinctness colors their perception and gives rise to a feeling. And though these feelings appear in manifold ways, each has the same source. Thus they are not linked *in* time, but *across* time. They occupy the same space; they exhibit the same feeling in varied ways. In this way, the warrior, priest, and projection are identical: each represents the situation peculiar to the time. But the earth shakes beneath them.

Hard earth is softened as it billows under their feet. The iconoclast rises and swallows the triplets' ankles, knees, hips, and throat. In unison, they eke out a final phrase: *We thought of everyth—*

The three professed. The ground consumes. The dead will rise. And in this way, space and time meld.

6.

We have identified and affirm Adolf Hitler's goal: to unmask the Jew and its nefarious attempt to enslave and erase humanity — *for all time.* "[We face] the most infernal plot against the freedom of humanity that history has ever known," a defiant Goebbels declared after Stalingrad.[61] This plot is yet perpetrated by the Jews.

> People are increasingly recognizing the work of the Jews around the world. It does them no good to use parliaments and courts to protect their parasitic existence. It will not be long before the whole world cries out against [them].... In the Fifteenth Protocol of the Elders of Zion it is written: "When the king of the Jews receives the crown upon his holy head that Europe will offer him, he will become the patriarch of the entire world." The Jews have often been near that triumph,

just as they believe they are today.... The Jew will not be the *patriarch of the world*, but rather the *leper*, the *scum*, the *victim of his own criminal desires*....[62]

How can one be a *victim of his own criminal desires*? Julius Evola notes that

the overall cycle of democratic and capitalist civilization ... will eventually usher in the last collectivist phase, to which it has inadvertently opened the way. It is therefore logical that ... the main [subversive] current may turn against both [Jews and Masons], as if they were residues to be liquidated once and for all.[63]

The "criminal desires" mentioned here are represented by the insatiable drive, as in this case, among Jews and Masons to subvert the traditional culture of Europe and her progeny. In Evola's Frankenstein-esque view, the former's succumbing to the subversive tide it *itself* ushered in is the culminating irony to a tragicomic unfolding of history. The comedy is, of course, European complicity in its own demise.

Goebbels would no doubt take a different view, and one more in line with Serrano's: when "the [Jew] thinks he has achieved victory, we quickly find just the opposite happens: *the danger becomes ever greater*. He begins to fear for the end of his illusory existence."[64] The Jew becomes a victim of its own parasitism: it has, by its nature, bled the host dry and left itself without sustenance. "The Jew will always act consistently with his nature and racial instincts. He cannot do otherwise. Just like a potato beetle destroys potatoes, the Jew destroys nations and peoples."[65] The compulsion Goebbels and Serrano describe is quite different than Evola's "tide of history" interpretation. Ultimately, the disagreement is one of token, not one of type: the Jew succumbs in the end nonetheless. The question is whether or not an Aryan will be there to see the final solution.

Perhaps the Hitlerist *philosophy of nonetheless* can aid this vision. If this occurs or not depends largely on one's worldview: does one opt for an Evolan, more *political* interpretation of the world situation ("tide of history"), or does one see through a *spiritual* lens ("nature of things") à la the Hitlerists? There will always be a gulf between those who see the world in a spiritual, mystical way and those who do not. Evola's philosophy was never accepted by the Third Reich, and his misunderstanding of Hitler's aims undoubtedly contributed to this.[66] We can see the disparity in worldviews from one's interpretation of the *Protocols* Goebbels mentions.

"I have read *The Protocols of the Elders of Zion*," Hitler disclosed, "— it simply appalled me. The stealthiness of the enemy, and his ubiquity!" Rauschning retorted: "But ... the *Protocols* are a manifest forgery.... [They] can't possibly be genuine."[67] *Why not?* asked Hitler — *for if the Protocols were not true, then their intrinsic truth is all the more convincing.* Argentinian novelist Gustavo Martínez-Zuviría (Hugo Wast) echoed this sentiment, saying, "The *Protocols* may well be a fake, but their predictions have been fulfilled in an amazing way"; Henry Ford shared a similar view:

> The only comment I can make about the *Protocols* is that they perfectly correspond to what is happening today. They were published sixteen years ago [in 1903], and ever since then they have corresponded to the world situation and today they still dictate its rhythm.[68]

Historicity is the plaything of the Jews — it is an arm of the information-dominance weapon they have so long wielded; that is, they can bend history to meet their needs and warp present realities through its obfuscation. What the abovementioned men are saying is, *if you want truth, look at reality — and stop listening to the purveyors of "history."* Even Evola was induced to agree: "the value of the [*Protocols*] as a working hypothesis is undeniable: it presents the various aspects of global subversion in terms of a whole, in which they find their sufficient reason and logical combination."[69] However, being the *nonexistent right's* version of a spinster, Evola couldn't help but play devil's advocate: "We may even wonder whether a fanatical anti-Semitism, which always sees the Jew as a *deus ex machina*, is not unwittingly playing into the hands of the enemy."[70]

To this the Hitlerist can only say: We are *all* playing into the hands of the enemy! To be sure, Evola admits as much when he concludes,

> despite the fact that many Jews are among the apostles of the main ideologies regarded by the *Protocols* as instruments of global subversion (i.e., liberalism, socialism, scientism, and rationalism), it is also evident that these ideas would have never arisen and triumphed without historical antecedents, such as the Reformation, Humanism, the naturalism and individualism of the Renaissance, and the philosophy of Descartes....[71]

He means to say that "the enemy" had help in reaching the summit — Evola is correct: the *White Traitor* is everywhere. But even this notion of the "White Traitor" is misleading, for it presupposes that there is some "white" (racial) solidarity from which to break away. There isn't. Instead, what exists is a "white" *Idea*, a "white" *culture*, a "white" *character*. Each of us interprets this Idea, from which culture and character flow, in his own way, which is precisely the Aryans' greatest strength and most devastating weakness; the only remedy to this is to base one's Idea on *faith* — a faith that reflects the Good, which stands as "that which transcends and uplifts; it is sacrificing oneself for the benefit of the whole that reflects oneself; this reflection is physical, mental, and spiritual..."[72] That is, the Idea must be Hitlerist, or all is lost.

7.

Evola references "forces that may have employed modern Judaism merely as an instrument" as an alternative to any "fanatical anti-Semitism" that strives to reveal the Jew. These forces protect themselves by "directing their opponents' attention toward those who are only partially responsible for certain upheavals."[73] Evola marks these forces as *democratism* and *capitalism*, the former essentially driving the latter. One can certainly see how these forces might be identified as drivers for modern degeneracy, but these are tools rather than prime movers. The mover must be something that implements the tool for an advantage. Adolf Hitler discerned the Jew; because of his incisiveness, we quote Hitler at length here:

> The political emancipation of the Jews was the beginning of an attack of delirium. For thereby they were given full citizen-rights and equality, and this to a people which was much more clearly and definitely a race apart than all others...
>
> And it was precisely the same in the economic sphere. The vast process of the industrialization of the peoples meant the confluence of great masses of workmen in the towns.... Parallel with this was a gradual *moneyfication* of the whole of the nation's workforce. "Share-capital" [ascended until], bit by bit, the *stock exchange* came to control the whole national economy.
>
> The directors of these institutions were, and are without exception, Jews. I say "without exception," for the few non-Jews who had a share in them are in the last resort nothing but screens, shop-window [Gentiles], whom one needs in order, for the sake of the masses, to keep up the appearance that these institutions were after all founded as a natural outcome of the needs and the economic life of all peoples alike, and were not, as was the fact, institutions which correspond only with the essential characteristics of the Jewish people and are the outcome of those characteristics....
>
> The masterstroke of the Jew was to claim the leadership of the fourth estate: he founded both the Social-Democratic and Communist movements. His policy was twofold: he had his "apostles" in both political camps. Amongst the parties of the Right he encouraged those features that were most repugnant to the people — the passion for money... And the Jew attacked the parties of the Right. Jews wormed their way into the families of the upper classes: it was from the Jews that the latter took their wives. The result was that in a short time it was precisely the ruling class

that became in its character completely estranged from its own people.

And this fact gave the Jew his opportunity with the parties of the Left. Here he played the part of the common demagogue. Two means enabled him to drive away in disgust the whole intelligentsia of the nation from the leadership of the workers. First: his international attitude—for the native intelligence of the country is prepared to make sacrifices; it will do anything for the life of the people, but it cannot believe in the mad view that ... through the breaking down of the national resistance to the foreigner, it is possible to elevate a people and make it happy. That it cannot do, and so it remained at a distance.

And the Jew's second instrument was the Marxist theory itself. For directly one went on to assert that property as such is theft; directly one deserted the obvious formula that only the natural wealth of a country can and should be common property, but what a man creates or gains through his honest labor is his own. Immediately the economic intelligentsia with its nationalist outlook could, here too, no longer cooperate: for this intelligentsia was bound to say ... that this theory meant the collapse of any human civilization whatever. Thus the Jew succeeded in isolating this new movement of the workers from all the nationalist elements.

The Jew agitated the masses evermore frequently, persuading those of the Right that the faults of the Left were the faults of the German workman, and similarly he made it appear to those of the Left that the faults of the Right were simply the faults of the so-called *bourgeoisie*. Meanwhile, neither side noticed that the faults of each were the result of a scheme planned by satanic, alien agitators. And only in this way is it possible to explain how this perverted joke of world history could come to be — that Stock-Exchange Jews should become the leaders of a workers movement. It is a gigantic fraud, and world history has seldom seen its like.[74]

All are encouraged to read this speech in its entirety (28 July 1922), as it is a landmark of sociopolitical discourse; it captures precisely the growth of the *ferment of decomposition.*[75]

Evola and his ilk, on the other hand, indicate the nebulous Third and Fourth Estates as the mover (i.e., if they do not indicate the implemented forces themselves as movers). The masses exist to be molded and moved; they are not movers. Forces can certainly mold and move the masses, but the forces must be in the hands of capable movers.

If Evola's "traditions" or "aristocracy" are under attack, unwielded forces are not attacking them — "Judaism" cannot be deployed "merely as an instrument."[76] Instead, it must be the movers who have made it their mission to degrade, usurp, and demolish the folk of Europe; it must be the Jews. This does not necessarily mean "the leaders of the great conflicting powers ... receive orders from an international center of Jews and Masons."[77] It rather means, as Serrano tells us, that Jews act with "the automatism of the anti-blood, the genetic code that [conditions] them to fulfill the *archetypical plan.*"[78] Jews act through a "Collective Unconscious [reminiscent of] a 'hydra with a thousand heads,' something without a center, or with an ubiquitous nature, omnipotent."[79] Nevertheless, the Jews could be preparing the way for their foul Messiah

> in the synagogues and lodges, a species of monstrous *Golem*, without blood, an arithmetic entity, imaginary, cybernetic, trans-infinite. Perhaps he could even have an electronic brain, a robot, which they manipulate. Nor can we exclude the installation of a Jewish Pope in Rome. Everything is still possible at these heights of the fulfillment of the millennial plan.[80]

The end approaches *nonetheless.*

8.

The modern notion of *accelerationism* can be traced to Nietzsche: "The *leveling* of the mankind of Europe is the great process which should not be arrested; it should even be accelerated."[81] Nietzsche's view was that the mediocre — the rule — should be maintained to act as a constant reference for the exception(al):

> It is precisely because [one] is the exception that he must protect the rule and ingratiate all mediocre people. [...] understanding that the continued existence of the rule is the first condition of the value of the exception.[82]

Thus, to ensure the best, the flaming heap of the least must be fanned. This certainly sounds like *winning by losing* — from the materialists' view, at least. From Nietzsche's perspective, however, it is the only way to "win." Without the dreck, there can be no beacon.

This, too, sounds similar to Hitler's view: "Two worlds face one another — the men of God and the men of Satan! The Jew is the anti-man, the creature of another god.... I set the Aryan and the Jew over against each other..."[83] Light and dark dance to bring life: this is the dance of Shiva. A year, a month, a day — each has its half of light and dark; there is spark and there is reprieve — each, in fulfilling its duty, never stops; it is only the harmony of the heavenly spheres which brings life to one, annihilation of the other. Aryan and Jew are antipode to each other: in a world of only Aryans — in blood and character — there would be but light[84]; in a world of only Jews — in blood and character — there would be but darkness and void[85]; the world in which Aryans and Jews coexist, however, gives us the Cosmic Struggle; it is the divine dance that brings life to one, annihilation to the other.

We are given in this struggle the meaning that brings us closer to God.[86] Fail to follow your duty, Aryan, and you are only fodder for the satanic urge, the Lord of Darkness: "Death is the oven that cooks the Demiurge's food. Material dissolves into material, energy revolves, transforms, and from pain there rises thick vapors that strengthen him."[87] The Jews fulfill their cosmic duty — wittingly or not — by ceaselessly striving for destruction of the Aryan and enslavement of the Gentile, *for all time*. But their abhorrent plan is *necessary* — so that the Aryan might fulfill his duty: final destruction of the Judeo-system and Jehovah's Infernal Return. Serrano continues:

> Here is something diabolical and terrible, an involution already seemingly impossible to detect. Studying bees, ants, and especially the natural life of termites, if one can call it that, we are terrified to think where man can end up; animal-men, and together with them the imprisoned *Vîras*, involuted Gods. There all individuality ends, including intelligence and personal freedom. There is nothing but continuous labor, reproduction and death. [It is the] obligatory sacrifice and misery of many for the unhappiness of all. And in the end: only food for the Demiurge.
>
> But was it always like that with the termites? They also show an initial intelligence that once was like a first impulse that planned this perfect organization, perhaps of only one individual or an elite that then disappeared, with nothing left remaining other than the automatism. It may be that the termites, ants, bees, many millions of years ago in other *Manvantaras*, were also Gods, divine beings, who were made prisoners by the Demiurge, becoming involuted into what they actually are now. And so it would be possible also for the animal-men of today and even for the imprisoned *Vîras* themselves, the White Traitors, those Aryan collaborators with the Demiurge, to be transformed into ants before this *Yuga* ends, reduced in physical size, as already imagined by the Jewish writer Kafka....
>
> Among ants and termites, individual intelligence and initiative is a crime paid for with immediate destruction. In the collectivist Marxist societies they tried to achieve the same state.... But the creators of such a society no longer need the Marxist experiment. That was a calculation of the Jewish *Kahal* [*Qahal*], where

the beings of that community are controlled from birth to death, directed moreover by only mechanical genetics, or the genetics of mechanics.[88]

Aryans have nothing to lose and everything to gain in this Cosmic Struggle. The future under the Judeo-system is an everlasting night. The die has already been cast; the Norns have spoken: the future has already been realized — it is bereft of Aryan spirit, and the Jew reigns supreme. What remains is the individual decision to fulfill a divine duty — a free will whose only function is to feel the fate that binds it.

Nietzsche understood that fate binds all: "... *live in danger!* Build your cities on the slope of Vesuvius! Send your ships into unexplored seas! Live in war with your equals and with yourselves!"[89] This constitutes the Nietzschean *amor fati* — love of fate.[90] It is fate that drives the Cosmic Struggle because it is fate that governs the Germanic people. The *Edda* speaks often of fate. In "Fafnismol," Sigurth describes Aryan courage: "I shall not flee, though my fate be near, I was born not a coward to be; Thy loving word for mine will I win, as long as I shall live."[91] Sigurth doesn't speak about *how long* he shall live, but only about *how he will fight* for as long as he lives. Likewise, Helgi reminds us: "the fighter can shun not his fate."[92]

Amor fati means we *participate* in the struggle — we do not forfeit our life to woeful, pathetic doldrums, nor do we plod along in the "metapolitical" arena hoping to change the hearts and minds that hardly exist. Participating in the struggle means we fight for righteousness — we fight for *one thing*, for meaning.[93] For the Hitlerist, this means accelerationism. Do nothing and watch an everlasting night envelop the termite mound of humanity; act — *participate in the struggle* — and honor what remains of the blood in your veins. We stake our claim on the slopes of Vesuvius because it reveals our *devotion to the struggle*, and not because we anticipate any material benefit; life on the Vesuvian slopes fulfills the heroic cycle wherein "sacrifice undergirds heroism [and] heroes are both a reflection of a people and a challenge to untested generations to continue the struggle."[94]

1 — Accelerationism and the Judeo-System

The *Edda* reminds us "the destined day shall come ... when every man shall journey ... to hell."[95] Should we abandon the struggle because we know it is hard? "For a tree to become GREAT, it seeketh to twine hard roots around hard rocks!"[96] Should we seek the gentler, more hospitable environs far away from death-dealing Vesuvius? This would amount to a rejection of the divine dance, a spurning of sacred duty. Certainly, one can choose this path; but it reveals only that one was lost from the start and that choice was never present, that one was only ever food for the Demiurge.[97]

We may learn again from Nietzsche:

> As men of the future, we thrust our roots always more powerfully into the deep — into evil —, while at the same time we embrace the heavens ever more lovingly, more extensively, and suck in their light ever more eagerly with all our branches and leaves.[98]

To be a *man of the future* means smashing the shackles of the Judeo-present; it means embracing the "barbarism" of our ancestors who themselves arose from an even more perilous time — a time which becomes our future and, soon, our present.

When Nietzsche mentions "evil" he means that which contravenes the present Judeo-ethical system — whether that system is seen through the lens of Judeo-materialism, Judeo-Marxism, or Judeo-Christianity. If the debauched system sees its cessation as "evil," we can be assured this cessation is, in fact, good. Nietzsche, above all, believed in a set of values that would shatter the looming lassitude of a mechanical, choice-less existence delivered to man from the mind of the Jew.

> For Nietzsche, "it was, in fact, with the Jews that the *revolt of the slaves* begins in the sphere *of morals*." Indeed, "it was the Jews who [stood] in opposition to the aristocratic equation (good = aristocratic = beautiful = happy = loved by the gods)" and it was "the Jews, [who effected] a radical transvaluation of values, which was at the same time an act of the *cleverest revenge*." Re-

venge against whom? Against "the conquering and *master* race — the Aryan race" of course! Needless to say, Nietzsche laments the inferiorizing effects the Jewish transvaluation of values has on the Germanic man. It is only through a stern devotion to a will to power that the Abrahamic revision of history can be upturned and demolished.[99]

The Aryan must stop hiding from his fate: his sole purpose in this Cosmic Struggle is the final solution to the Jewish Question: it is the annihilation of the Judeo-system — *for all time*. This cannot be done through political scheming, through playing the Jews' game in the Jews' system. The "final battle, in which fire and flood overwhelm heaven and earth as the gods fight with their enemies, is the *great fact* in Norse mythology; the phrase describing it, *ragna rök*, 'the fate of the gods,' has become familiar..."[100] — not familiar enough, it seems; though it will become more familiar than even the mien in the mirror.

The *great fact* of Aryan mythology is the prophecy that defines our future; and it is the prelude from which the prophecy is derived. All has already happened; we have only to feel — *to live* — the fate that binds our will to its ineluctable end.

9.

What is it you cling to, Aryan? What is it that stays your hand and stills your will? Do you fear the latent flame lurking in the smoldering masses? Shiva waits for *you*; his dance is the fire your destiny demands. Is it possible the fanned flames get "out of control"? *Yes* — living on the slopes of Vesuvius is a necessary danger to stimulate the best — i.e., victory. And *yes* — Shiva is beyond control; *ragna rök*, "the fate of the gods," is beyond control. *Control* is a figment of the Judeo-system; it is the emotive tether habituating you to subservience under the Jewish heel. *Control, produce, consume, ... submit* — all are synonymous in the Judeo-context. *Resist just a little more, comrades,* as Don Serrano beseeched. You are but a part of the Cosmic Struggle; the Struggle itself is divine *diktat*, which is the fate your future self has irrepressibly embraced.

And though it is fate that drives all, it is faith that offers meaning. VAL'HALLA — ALLAH'LAV: The halls of Valhalla were known and sought by Aryans from the earliest days of Wotan. The aspirant struggles to transmute a life of suffering into a life of glory, honor, and loyalty (*Meine Ehre heißt Treue*): This faith in the Good[101] is the difference between a mere will-to-live and the vigorous will-to-power — though the power sought is not one of *exploitation*, but one of *communion*: the gods await at the end of the struggle to attach meaning to one's lineage. The Aryans were and are, to what extent they remain, a duty-bound people. The struggle for honor and loyalty is a fight for the blood in one's veins.

One who battles through life to attain Valhalla doesn't then revert to a mere will-to-live — the hero is not content to enjoy the lavish halls; rather, he daily *exits* the hall doors, fights to the death, revels in the glory, and lives to do it all again — *for all time*. This is the Aryan covenant with the gods: Make your folk proud and earn your place among the pantheon through honor and loyalty.

Such divine duty, such vigor stands both in stark contrast to and was overtaken by worldly treasure, by the Jewish covenant with the Lord of Darkness. Through a fundamental and world-shattering disloyalty, powerful Aryans forsook their spiritual-cultural duty for shiny metals, extravagance, and a hollow piousness: in this way, they debased their divinity until it only nominally existed, which marked the end of the Aryan Führers (spiritual-aristocracy) and the beginning of the Aryan Monarchs (material-aristocracy).[102] The monarchs were to be a puppet for the Jews, paving the way to parliamentarianism, which would grant them full rights in heretofore exclusively Aryan lands.

The greatest example of this yet exists in a once-great Aryan stronghold, England — Angle-Land; the "constitutional monarchy" is played out daily in the blackening of the "white" nation and the City of London money-trading; non-Aryan political leaders are installed over formerly Aryan people to further debase them. This "divide and conquer" game is familiar to the "British" — i.e., the corporate empire that was so easily overcome by the Jewish spirit. "Enlisting the sympathy of one [side] to put down the other"[103] is what the Brits have done, perhaps better than anyone, for centuries. Whether in India, Burma, the American colonies, or elsewhere, British policy was to foment and exploit discord among indigenous peoples to maximize the thrust of their inferior numbers: encourage competition for favor here, sow infighting there — the result was and is always the same: make them grovel and pilfer their stockpiles through statecraft and City-of-London usury. All in good time will the Jewish spirit completely devastate the *Angle-Land*; all in good time will *Angle-Land* move from mere playground of the Jews to processing- and triaging-canton for noncompliant Aryans.

When the Aryans were still honorable and loyal, they spread across the globe, carrying their culture with them. Ruins of ancient "civilizations" bespeak such diffusion, and many have spoken of these connections elsewhere. Of note here, however, is the link between the Aryan *Valhalla* and the Arabic *Allah*. Of Germanic origin, *Valhalla* (*val'hǫll*) translates to "hall of the slain." *Hall* (*Halle*) is also of Germanic origin, being the gathering place for the tribal chief and his folk. Likewise, *the slain*, derived from *to slay* (*slaan* or *schlagen*), is Germanic, meaning *to kill* or *to strike*. Thus, those who live honorably in life (the fighters) meet honor in death in the form of sitting with their "tribal chief," the gods in the halls of Valhalla. *Allah'lav*, or more precisely, *Allah(i)law*, translates to "hallelujah" in Arabic, or "God bless" in Farsi ("God love"). One is indeed blessed by the gods if he earns a spot next to them. *God is great*. This wordplay will perhaps be dismissed as folk etymology, but words come from the folk; Farsi and the Germanic languages share space on the Indo-European tree — their roots are with the Aryans. *The God* (*Allah*) perhaps came from the north with the conquering Aryan, but it became the monolithic ONE with the Semitic influence of the Levantine world.

Iranian (*Aryanian*) Ruhollah Khomeini, himself a user of the word *Allah*, said,

> We must protest and make the people aware that the Jews and their foreign backers ... wish to establish Jewish domination throughout the world. Since they are a cunning and resourceful group of people, I fear that — *God forbid!* — they may one day achieve their goal, and

that the apathy shown by some of us may allow a Jew to rule over us one day. May God never let us see such a day![104]

Far beyond any supposed etymological link (or lack thereof) is the spiritual-cultural root that binds two peoples together. Where they find common ground is in their recognition of the Jewish problem. Listen well, Aryan: Do you wish to commune with God and fulfill your divine duty? Solve the Jewish problem *for all time.*

The day Khomeini feared is indeed here: if we Gentiles are not ruled by a blood-Jew, we are certainly all ruled by spirit-Jews, by collaborators hitching themselves to Judeo-coattails on the ascent up the anthill of material-aristocracy. But there is a solution: *dance with Shiva*, topple the Judeo-system, *dispossess the Jew of the material basis that is its essence*, fulfill your part in the Cosmic Struggle and solve the Jewish problem — *for all time.*

10.

Ted Kaczynski, whatever one thinks of his methods — *and who are we to judge atop this lukewarm anthill?* —, was correct in his survey of the present situation:

> There is no way of reforming or modifying the system so as to prevent it from depriving people of dignity and autonomy. If the system breaks down, the consequences will still be very painful. But the bigger the system grows the more disastrous the results of its breakdown will be, so if it is to break down it had best break down sooner rather than later.... We therefore advocate a revolution against the industrial system.... This is not to be a POLITICAL revolution.[105]

The lukewarm will protest this assessment and the deeds it demands. This is because the lukewarm seek — largely for selfish reasons — a political solution; naturally, then, they are repulsed by any non-political solution. We should never forget that those seeking a political solution are infested with the *ferment of decomposi-*

tion — i.e., the Jewish spirit: they are the Judeo-bot, the Zombie-Jew, the "conservative" Judeo-Christian, the privileged bourgeois, the husk hoping not to be engulfed in Shiva's redemptive flames. *Why destroy the whole system when there's profit to be made?* — this is what the lukewarm think, and they blink. "*We have discovered happiness* — say the last men, and blink thereby." Who are the last men? "His species is ineradicable like that of the ground-flea; the last man liveth longest."[106] The "last men" are no different than the Judeo-system they hold so dear. *Ineradicable?* We would do well to eradicate them *nonetheless*.

11.

Jünger often spoke of the *worker*: "What role does pain play in the new race we have called the *worker* that is now making its appearance on the historical stage?"[107] The *worker* is the post-individual being that arises to meet the failings of the liberalistic system; he is a part of the whole, the "new race" both at home in and transcending the materialistic autonomy of the "old cults." The *worker* is the living part of a technicized entity bent on destroying the very technical foundations undergirding it; first comes destruction of the individual self, then comes the end of the *technicizing* process-structure that obliterates the self. The *worker* is therefore a parallel dismantling of the status quo ("old cults") and the individual that emerges to rebel against it. The *worker* is submission to authority — not to any material authority, but to a spiritual *diktat* that demands subsumption and subservience — or not.

Prior to the revolutionary era of the twentieth century, the worker was not possible because *offense* was not possible — i.e., the offense that "both reveals and obscures the revelation; as revelation, the offense unmasks those who would do the truth harm; as obscuration, the offense is an inability to adjudge the Avatāra because of a separation from God and the humanity that elevated our spirit to the heights of history."[108] Offense was not possible because the individual in the liberal-individualistic society melted into oblivion — all was lost in a sea of non-sea; it was as if the sea itself had vaporized into a blanketing mist from the red-hot embers of the scorched *ancien régime*. The Enlightenment and its subsequent liberal revolutions, far from spawning societies of freethinkers, birthed instead an ethereal haze of conformity that still clouds our vision today.

Jünger saw a new race, a race that would obliterate — *for all time* — the dispassionate non-entities born of the liberal era. It is perhaps believed that the anti-liberalistic revolutionary whirlwind of the twentieth century dissipated in 1945, but this was just the *beginning*. The future does not hold political revolution, however, but the liberating transcendence of submission to the ultimate authority: the inner voice of conscience freed from good and evil — i.e., the voice of God.

What does God say? *Bring down the Judeo-system!* You are the tools you use, just as they are you. Welcome the oneness with the implement: self and implement are forged into a divine will that cannot fail to clear the fog of material-aristocracy and the conformity it requires. The crescendo of whispers you hear on the other side of Shiva is not a utopia of fellow travelers; it is an ancestral resonance pleased with the sacrifice that gave rise to you; it is the condensation of hovering mist into roaring sea, and the breaking of the waves under the ship of sacrifice carrying you to Valhalla.

12.

We could never exist in a world where monuments to righteousness were erected: no statues of Adolf Hitler, Rudolf Hess, Hans-Ulrich Rudel, Otto Skorzeny, Léon Degrelle, Savitri Devi, and Miguel Serrano are possible. It's not simply that they *do not* exist but *could* — it's that they are *not possible*, for the world they envisioned transcends the world that bore them. A world ruled by the Lord of Darkness cannot bear witness to the Sons and Daughters of Light. No, the tribute we pay to Light does not manifest materially; respect is shown in the sacrifices we make. We are animated by faith and recognize the advantage in sacrifice: Our towers are new, and they reach the heavens in pillars of smoke.

A monument can only exist when sacrifice is absent. When sacrifice is replaced by hardened material, such a monument is only a promise of future ruin. And what is *politics* if not a monument to ruin, what are the halls of parliament if not the secular tombs of God?[109] Politics is an augur of the age and seal of the cataclysm to come.

"Moderation at all costs"?[110] *No* — accelerationism against all odds, *nonetheless*!

Accelerationism and the Judeo-System — Notes

[1] Carl Schmitt, *Political Theology* (2005), 66.
[2] "Our imperialism must spring forth from a deep confidence in the victory of righteousness." Ernst Jünger, "The Frontline Soldier," *Die Standarte* (September 1925).
[3] Hermann Rauschning, *The Voice of Destruction* (1940), 241-242.
[4] 28 July 1922 (speech); emphasis added. See T. Dalton's *Hitler on the Jews* (2019) for extended passages.
[5] Jünger, "The Frontline Soldier."
[6] See fn8 below.
[7] Martin Friedrich, *Hitler Avatāra* (2023), 10, 61, 71, 99.
[8] "Positive political change won't come from destruction.... Metapolitics [sic] is the way we will return to healthy ethnocentrism ... [even though] *we don't have the same resources* as those who indoctrinated and continue to indoctrinate our people..." — so says one "ethnocentrist" ("South Africa Discredits 'Accelerationism,'" [Counter Currents, 09 August 2023]). And another "ethnocentrist": "[In 2016] we wanted Trump to win the election and then triumph over ... the *deep state*.... [At this time] it became clear to me that accelerationism had mutated ... into a toxic 'strategy' that basically amounts to the axiom that 'We win by losing.' It would have been perfectly understandable to advance such ideas if Trump had actually lost. But when our ideas were actually threatening to win out, it was the height of perversity to suggest that we snatch defeat from the jaws of victory because we somehow win by losing.... [A]ctually we lose by losing. When we lose, we can of course hope that somehow the gods or 'history' will turn our defeats into conditions for future victories. But in the end, we can only win by winning" (Greg Johnson, "Against Accelerationism," [Counter Currents, 06 January 2020]). Both commentators allude to some kind of *material, political victory* — this, despite an acknowledgement from each that a sociopolitical system stocked with incomprehensible resources is pit against them (see added emphasis in the foregoing quotations).
[9] Ernst Jünger, *The Worker* (2017), §1.
[10] T. Kaczynski, *Unabomber In His Own Words* (2020), part 3, 24:37.
[11] Savitri Devi, *Gold in the Furnace* (1952), "The Elite of the World." Savitri quotes *Mein Kampf*.
[12] Leon Trotsky, *The Revolution Betrayed* (2004), 120; emphasis added.
[13] *Melting Pot* (1908) was a play written by the Jew Israel Zangwill. His play was lauded by the Judeo-system (Theodore Roosevelt is said to have praised the production after attending its opening night; see

Rochelson, *A Jew in the Public Arena* [2008], xxiii, 180-81); "melting pot" subsequently assumed popular use.

[14] F.P. Yockey, *Imperium* (1948), "Subjective Meaning of Race," I. See also "Race, People, Nation, State" (IV) in the same work.

[15] Adolf Hitler, *Second Book*, ch. 3; emphasis added.

[16] For a more detailed discussion of faith, race, and the restoration of right — or, "winning by losing" — see Friedrich, *Hitler Avatāra*.

[17] Ernst Jünger, "Differentiation and Connection," *Die Standarte* (September 1925). Jünger, who is not impugning Hitlerists here, often has this sentiment appropriated by various members of the "right" to defend their politicking.

[18] Miguel Serrano, *Adolf Hitler: The Ultimate Avatar* (2014), 236; emphasis added.

[19] Ernst Jünger, "Revolution and the Idea," *Völkischer Beobachter* (September 1923).

[20] Søren Kierkegaard, *Training in Christianity* (2004), 83. See also *Hitler Avatāra*.

[21] Perhaps only a Jew would save a fellow sordid Jew — just because it was a "fellow Jew," character be damned. Judeo-racialism, *Judeo-materialism* knows no bounds.

[22] Arthur Möller van den Bruck, *Das Dritte Reich* (2012), 83.

[23] Miguel Serrano, *NOS: Book of the Resurrection* (1984), 130.

[24] An exchange in the *New York Review* (Barr and Baruma, 16 December 1993) notes that Jünger "agreed with most of Hitler's aims until 1938. As he told *Der Spiegel*, he went along with Hitler's opposition to the Versailles Treaty and his annexations of Austria and the Sudetenland. He only condemned Hitler's 'flagrant injustice after 1938.'" That is, he supported Hitler until it became apparent that Poland's relationship with Germany would be dealt with next (1939). Jünger saw the writing on the wall in the propaganda run-up to the invasion of Poland and, more pragmatically, reckoned that the doors of Europe would irrevocably shut on Germany should it act on its judgments regarding Poland. Hitler, as is apparent, was committed to his plan of consolidating all former German territories and Germanic peoples under the Swastika; he showed little regard for the material consequences of his actions. Jünger, on the other hand, was willing to let his nationalistic passions cool for the sake of Germany's survival. Herein lies the difference between Hitler and Jünger: Adolf Hitler was *willing to sacrifice everything* — to include survival — for the *Idea*; Ernst Jünger was willing to sacrifice up to the point of extermination (not of self, but of *Gemeinschaft*). Which man best embodies the Nietzschean philosophy, then? Only the man who speaks and acts for the coming millennia: Adolf Hitler. One

suspects that for Hitler, the *Gemeinschaft* would essentially cease to exist if its foundational passions had to be sacrificed for its own preservation; that is, what one would hope to preserve by half measures would be unworthy of preservation at all — "These mediators and mixers we detest — the passing clouds: those *half-and-half ones*, that have neither learned to bless nor to curse from the heart" (Nietzsche, *Thus Spoke Zarathustra*, Part III, "Before Sunrise").

25 "Blood," *Die Standarte* (April 1926).
26 Serrano, *Adolf Hitler*, 297; emphasis added.
27 01 January 1933 (speech); emphasis added.
28 See both *Hitler Avatāra* and *Myth and Sun* (2022).
29 Greg Johnson, "Against Accelerationism," (Counter Currents, 06 January 2020): "[W]e can only win by winning."
30 Jünger, "The Frontline Soldier."
31 Ernst Jünger, "The Machine," *Die Standarte* (December 1925).
32 Adolf Hitler, 01 January 1933 (speech).
33 Serrano, *Adolf Hitler*, 763.
34 Serrano, *Adolf Hitler*, 840.
35 "The cycle of time ensures that future weak men will eventually re-sow these seeds; and they, like us, will grapple with their tenuous survival" (*Myth and Sun*, 317).
36 "Theirs [is] not to reason why, Theirs [is] but to do and die," Alfred Tennyson, "The Charge of the Light Brigade."
37 From the ELF's first, anonymous communiqué.
38 "[A]ccelerationist violence is a nihilist symptom attacking alienating social conditions perceived to be unjust" (M. Loadenthal, "Feral fascists and deep green guerrillas: infrastructural attack and accelerationist terror," *Critical Studies on Terrorism*, 15:1 [2022], 199). How, precisely, is it possible that a "nihilist" would care to attack "injustice"? *Perceiving*, let alone *attacking*, injustice indicates a distinct *lack* of nihilistic tendencies. This somewhat inconceivable misperception is akin to the intellectually lazy branding of Hitlerists as "Satanists" (Loadenthal, 200), which arises from a system that has been Judaized to the point of Pavlovian response to the (light-bringing, Aryan) "Lucifer" contravening the Jehovahistic (i.e., satanic, anti-Aryan) system. Both misunderstandings stem from either deliberate misinformation or intellectual laziness. Regardless of the source, more Judaization is the result.
39 Jünger, "On Spirit," *Widerstand* (April 1927).
40 From Goebbels' pamphlet (originally distributed in 1929), "Die verfluchten Hakenkreuzler" ("Those Damned Hooked-Crossers," 1932); emphasis added.

41 Rauschning, *The Voice of Destruction*, 246. Similarly quoted in Serrano's *Manu: For the Man to Come* (2017), and in *Morning of the Magicians* (Louis Pauwels and Jacques Bergier; 1973), 256.
42 Hermann Rauschning, *Germany's Revolution of Destruction* (1940), 13 and 62; emphasis added.
43 Rauschning seemed to have really believed that the Hitlerian Movement was something of a world-swallowing black hole growing, already in 1936, at an alarming rate and, moreover, one that needed to be quelled. While he didn't recognize it, his concern was not for any nihilistic tendencies within the Movement, but rather that Rauschning's own platform was under attack. To mitigate the popular swell rising behind Hitler, Rauschning took to sensationalizing events as he saw them; hence the somewhat dubious nature of Rauschning's work.
44 If this sword is double-edged, then perhaps it means the world will burn regardless, which indeed it will.
45 Kierkegaard, *Fear and Trembling* (1983), 55.
46 Or "absolute duty to God": Kierkegaard, *Fear and Trembling*, 70.
47 *Beyond Good and Evil*, §153.
48 Kierkegaard, *Fear and Trembling*, 44.
49 Kierkegaard describes *infinite resignation* as a necessary *antecedent* to faith (*Fear and Trembling*, op. cit., 47), but we should not think of this step as utterly *distinct* from the movement to faith anymore than we would think evaporation is distinct from the condensation of water vapor in the atmosphere.
50 Jünger, "On Spirit."
51 Daniel Byman, "Riots, white supremacy, and accelerationism" (02 June 2020).
52 28 July 1922 (speech).
53 Rauschning, *The Voice of Destruction*, 252.
54 *Origins and Doctrine of Fascism* (2005), 45-46; emphasis added.
55 See *Myth and Sun*, "Foundations for a Healthy Society."
56 *Political Testament* (1812).
57 See Nietzsche, *Thus Spoke Zarathustra*, Part I, "Zarathustra's Prologue" and fn96 below.
58 See *Myth and Sun* and *Hitler Avatāra*.
59 *On Pain* (2008), §16.
60 *On Pain*, §1.
61 05 June 1943 (speech).
62 Goebbels, 05 June 1943 (speech). See T. Dalton's *Goebbels on the Jews* (2019) for extended passages.
63 *Men Among the Ruins* (2002), 243.
64 *Manu*, 177.

⁶⁵ Goebbels, 05 June 1943 (speech).
⁶⁶ The fact that Evola is so esteemed by the *sophisticated ethnocentrists* of the nonexistent "right" is an historical curiosity and impressive sign of the times.
⁶⁷ Rauschning, *The Voice of Destruction*, 238. See T. Dalton's *Protocols of the Elders of Zion: The Definitive English Edition* (2023).
⁶⁸ As quoted in *Men Among the Ruins*, 240.
⁶⁹ *Men Among the Ruins*, 240.
⁷⁰ *Men Among the Ruins*, 241.
⁷¹ *Men Among the Ruins*, 242.
⁷² *Hitler Avatāra*, 41 and 48.
⁷³ *Men Among the Ruins*, 242 and 241.
⁷⁴ Adolf Hitler, 28 July 1922 (speech).
⁷⁵ Theodor Mommsen, *The History of Rome* (1856/1871), 643.
⁷⁶ *Men Among the Ruins*, 242.
⁷⁷ *Men Among the Ruins*, 243.
⁷⁸ Serrano, *Adolf Hitler*, 88; emphasis added.
⁷⁹ Serrano, *Adolf Hitler*, 115.
⁸⁰ Serrano, *Adolf Hitler*, 104.
⁸¹ *The Will To Power* (2006), §898.
⁸² *The Will To Power*, §893, §894.
⁸³ Rauschning, *The Voice of Destruction*, 241-242.
⁸⁴ "[Aryans] are a solar race; but from that Sun which lies on the other side of all the suns. Our star is close by and appears to the Walkers of the Dawn to show them the way, beyond the Sun of Gold and the Black Sun, to the mansions of the Ray of Green Light, from whence love and dreaming come to us" (Serrano, *NOS*, 26).
⁸⁵ "If the Jew ... were to triumph over the people of this world, ... this planet will once again follow its orbit through the ether devoid of humanity, just as it did millions of years ago" (Adolf Hitler, *Mein Kampf* vol. 1 [2017], "Years of Studying and Suffering in Vienna," 153).
⁸⁶ This meaning is the faith that makes us authentic beings, discussed at length in *Hitler Avatāra*.
⁸⁷ Serrano, *Manu*, 73.
⁸⁸ Serrano, *Manu*, 191.
⁸⁹ Nietzsche, *Joyful Science*, §283.
⁹⁰ See Nietzsche, *The Will to Power* §1041 and *Joyful Science*, §276.
⁹¹ *Poetic Edda* (1936), "Fafnismol," §21.
⁹² *Poetic Edda*, "Helgakvitha Hjorvarthssonar," §21.
⁹³ See *Hitler Avatāra*, 41-43.
⁹⁴ *Hitler Avatāra*, 83.
⁹⁵ *Poetic Edda*, "Fafnismol," §10.

96 Nietzsche, *Thus Spoke Zarathustra*, Part III, "The Bedwarfing Virtue."
97 *Hitler Avatāra*, 86-87.
98 Nietzsche, *Joyful Science*, §371.
99 *Myth and Sun*, 285. The Nietzsche excerpts come from *On the Genealogy of Morals*, Essay I, §7.
100 Henry Adams Bellows, *Poetic Edda*, Introductory Note to "Voluspo"; emphasis added.
101 "The Good is that which transcends and uplifts; it is sacrificing oneself for the benefit of the whole that reflects oneself; this reflection is physical, mental, and spiritual; the Good is *one thing*" (*Hitler Avatāra*, 41 and 85).
102 See *Hitler Avatāra* for more on the concepts of spiritual and material aristocracies.
103 William Roger Louis et al., *The Oxford History of the British Empire: The Eighteenth Century* (1998), 519.
104 *Islamic Government*, translated by Hamid Algar.
105 Kaczynski, *Industrial Society and its Future*, paragraphs 2, 3, 4.
106 Nietzsche, *Thus Spoke Zarathustra*, Part I, "Zarathustra's Prologue."
107 *On Pain*, §1. See also, Jünger's *The Worker*.
108 *Hitler Avatāra*, 36.
109 Nietzsche, *Joyful Science*, §125: "What are these churches now, if they are not the tombs and monuments of God?"
110 Gentile, *Origins and Doctrine of Fascism*, 46.

— 2 —
Population and Technics

> *[The fighter] from time to time feels within the sleeping fires of a primitive soul. He feels the full pride of knowing oneself feared, admired, and hated for one's fortune and strength, and the urge to vengeance upon all, whether living beings or things, that constitute, if only by their mere existence, a threat to this pride.*
> — Oswald Spengler
> *Man and Technics*

1.

Carry danger within you. Make danger the *Schwerpunkt* of the struggle within yourself: Do you ignore destiny? Do you disparage passion? Are you offended? Is faith for backwater churners? *Destiny* is life. *Passion* sets the world afire. *Offense* is the key to faith. *Faith* is the language of world movers. And danger? *Danger* is the swelling of your chest, the clarity of your vision, the jaws of your boot: *God will come down upon you and you will die by the sword's edge!*[1] What you demand of others, you also live by. This is the crux of population and technics. Population is the mass; technics are the means. What is the end? The end is the world-burning fire that consumes man and machine.

Population

Two problems confront our time: the dreck and the Jew. Both survive and excel in the Judeo-system, for the Jew built a system in which it can thrive unmolested, if not undetected. The Jew's extensive *overt* meddling is a recent phenomenon stemming from the *Götterdämmerung* (1945). Jewish instinct is hiddenness, however — to orchestrate from the shadows; for it is in the shadows, spawned from the Lord of Darkness, that the Jew is most comfortable. The Jew is most attracted to reason, rationality, positivism, and scientism — "We own the science," says the UN Under-Secretary General for Global Communications.[2] This affinity for "reason" appeals to the Jewish proclivity for deception: much power resides in words, and silver tongues are often worth twice their weight in gold on the Jewish exchange.

In the end, "reason" is an indoctrinatory dogma, if not a ritualistic mantra, that the Jews and their allies disseminate through positions of authority and the mediums they control: media, medicine, finance, academia, and government.[3] This results in our current reality wherein, for example, the aforementioned UN Under-Secretary gushes about Jews welcoming refugees with open arms.[4] Of course, this single case encapsulates modernity: A hidden Jew uses her position of influence to rhapsodize the Jewish community welcoming non-European refugees into historically European lands. This is the confluence of population and technics, neither of which are in Aryan hands — nor will they ever be again in the Kali-Yuga.

Jacobins in Mercedes convertibles — this, meanwhile, is how the Jew Ben Stein characterizes his media brethren.[5] "A distinct majority [of media producers and writers] is Jewish…. [and] all [think] of themselves as politically 'progressive…'"[6] Their solution to what they see as *oppression* and *inequality* is found in "the redistribution of wealth … a complete scraping away of the ghettoes … [and] a rethinking of white supremacy." This is why in media nonwhites are portrayed as "utterly innocent," as "victimized by … social incompetence," and are "relieved of any responsibility … simply by not being shown doing anything bad." The media "[does] not hold [nonwhite] criminals responsible for crime but rather place[s] the blame on society" — this is a strange curiosity since the same media "believed … a person who was rich could largely thank himself for his riches, but a person who was poor could do no such thing." All of this is nothing more than Jewish subterfuge. And, ultimately, what pervades modern existence is only "the [Jewish] experience" disseminated across technological cages the world over.[7] Tellingly, Stein observes:

> [The people who make television] are [trying] to move their class to the top of the heap and to displace whatever stands in the way. By their intelligence and the power of technology, they stand astride the most

powerful media instrument of all time. This tiny community ... has been given the fulcrum that can move the world — and its members know how to use it.⁸

The convergence of population, technics, and Jew is the watershed separating man from the seas of the Divine.

2.

Politics is dead. Nietzsche has already foretold the "history of the next two centuries."⁹ What he augured is Nihilism. What politics can exist in a nihilistic world except slavery, the dynamic of *master* and *slave*? The *acrimonious* mastering the *apathetic*: this is the system imposed by the Jew to assure its ascent, and this system guarantees Jewish supremacy — for now. To fulfill Nietzsche's 200 years, we have yet to live six or seven more decades; we still talk of the cancer of liberalism; we still lament the placid and vapid existence of the "liberal bourgeois." We continue to discuss such things because we have not completed our nihilistic arc. What comes at the end of this arc? Those clingers-to-politics, the *liberal bourgeois* themselves, might imagine some new politics, wherein a "new order" is established. What "new order" can follow the Jew Order? *None* — for the Jew plants seeds of destruction, and the only harvest following the Season of the Jew is death. *Politics in the highest sense is life, and life is politics.*¹⁰ If life is politics and politics is dead, the languishing of modernity becomes clear.

Death is not our fear, but the Jew is our disgust. This is the new "politics" — the *anti-politics*, which is to say, the *anti-Jew*. Already "this Earth is ... a patient without remedy, without possible redemption; it is a dying body, where the microbes of the destruction of the corpse — the Jews — will perish with it."¹¹ Death is from Shiva; death is but part of Nature's cycle; we followers of Nature find solace in death. But this natural death is not what the Jew brings; rather, it brings a spiritual death, an oppression and annihilation of spirit and self. Without the self, the collective destiny, predicated on blood, cannot be fulfilled. If the collective destiny cannot be fulfilled, then communion with God is precluded.

The Jew is therefore the primeval disruptor and, moreover, the disruptor of the divine plan, which is to say, the Jew is anti-Nature; in short, the Jew is the *ferment of decomposition*. Do you seek life? Do you value natural growth and waning, life's natural ebb and flow? Because of its exploitative character, the Jew cannot provide this. Rather, the death imposed by Jewry is the *perpetual growth predicated on the debasement and enslavement of man — for all time*. The Judeo-system provides the parameters for this oppression and slavery. These parameters are *economics* and *mechanization*.

Economics, held Spengler, is "the *cause* and content of the world catastrophe."[12] It is the morphing of men into figures, digitized to death in a disappearing world. Mechanization is alienation; it is not only the means for economic ascent, but also the decoupling of man from humanity, whereby the lullabies of the Judeo-system's false prophets blanket the masses in delirium. Kaczynski presciently observed:

> Modern man is strapped down by a network of rules and regulations, and his fate depends on the actions of persons remote from him whose decisions he cannot influence. This is not accidental.... It is necessary and inevitable in any technologically advanced society. The system HAS TO regulate human behavior closely in order to function.... It may be, however, that *formal regulations will tend increasingly to be replaced by psychological tools that make us want to do what the system requires of us.* (Propaganda, educational techniques, "mental health" programs, etc.)....
>
> Most individuals are unable to influence measurably the major decisions that affect their lives. There is no conceivable way to remedy this in a technologically advanced society. *The system tries to "solve" this problem by using propaganda to make people WANT the decisions that have been made for them*, but even if this "solution" were completely successful in making people feel better, it would be demeaning....

> The system does not and cannot exist to satisfy human needs. Instead, it is *human behavior that has to be modified to fit the needs of the system.*... It is the fault of technology, because the system is guided ... by technical necessity.... *But the system ... must exert constant pressure on people to mold their behavior to the needs of the system.* Too much waste accumulating? The government, the media, the educational system, environmentalists, everyone inundates us with a mass of propaganda about recycling. Need more technical personnel? A chorus of voices exhorts kids to study science. No one stops to ask whether it is inhumane to force adolescents to spend the bulk of their time studying subjects that most of them hate.... It is simply taken for granted that *everyone must bow to technical necessity.*[13]

What Kaczynski describes as the *technological system* we call the *Judeo-system*, which is meant both to demean and increasingly restrict man's freedom. "The more complex modern technology becomes 'the more the apparatus grows into a self-sufficient being and the greater is the danger of a tyranny over human beings.' Means turn into ends. Technology escapes human control."[14] *Technology escapes human control* — this, of course, is the goal; superficial convenience and an increase in "quality" of life are not and never were the aim.

That technocratic intimations arise out of Enlightenment liberalism, which itself coincided with the emancipation of the Jews in Europe, can hardly be surprising. The apotheosization of technology, of *science*, was always intended to be a means to man's enslavement, the Kafkaesque metamorphosis of man into insect.[15] This system subtly achieves its objectives by incessant propaganda emanating from its panopticons of media, medicine, academia, finance, and government. "Propaganda is the executive arm of the invisible government."[16] This "government" is invisible because, neither elected nor appointed, it controls information directed at the citizenry — something the government proper does not "legally" have the authority to do[17] — and it controls the money and means necessary to promulgate dynamic mass propaganda; this it does through technological control.

Kaczynski does not identify the technological system with the Jew, but when we see the cupolas always filled with Jews and their allies, we cannot help but equate the two. Perhaps this equation is itself a product of the Kali-Yuga, with each side fulfilling its inescapable destiny, but it matters not. The end approaches nonetheless, and we must act according to the divine drive within us.

That the Jew is paramount and prevalent in this final age speaks volumes — the Jew telling you otherwise is itself a sign of the times. Barbara Lerner Spectre, founding director of the European Institute for Jewish Studies (Paideia), offered this typically Jewish assessment of Europe, for example, in an interview with Israel Broadcasting Authority (IBA) News circa 2011:

> Jews are going to be at the center of [the multicultural transformation of Europe that *must* take place]; it's a huge transformation for Europe to make; they are now going into a multicultural mode, and Jews will be resented because of our leading role. But without that leading role and without that transformation, Europe will not survive.

Jews are always at the center of societal upheaval — it is their diabolical purpose. Jews, like the puppet-governments they control, are quick to tell the masses that their efforts offer *stability* and *security* — and, in this case, even *survival*. However, *what survival can come from the spiritual-cultural destruction of an indigenous folk?* This illogic, wrapped in periphrasis, is the poison that drips from the jowls of the death-dealing Jew; when the Jew salivates, folk die. Jew *qua* Savior only ever means extinction or enslavement.

Kaczynski mentions the cavalcade of "important" talking heads and the disembodied voices one hears from all corners when the system wishes to steer public opinion. The recent Hamas-Israel confrontation illustrates the information sphere's saturation in the fallout of a pivotal event in the Judeo-plan. If one were a newcomer to this issue, to listen to the cascade of talking points one would think Hamas were comprised of devils and has the sole mission of killing precious Jewish babies — those future resentful meddlers who will inherit and advance the exploitative system co-created by their Jewish custodians and promised by their satanic pact with Jehovah.[18] The same lying propaganda was used against Germanic pagans to convert Europe to Christianity; it was used to rally the Germanic world around duplicitous popes for crusades meant to deplete European blood and enrich the Judeo-Christian Church; it was applied against the Aryan Russians when world Jewry deposed the czar and sought to heuristically trial the imposition of a global Judeo-system; it was deployed against the Germanic folk in two world wars[19] meant — again — to dishonor and diminish European blood forever.

All of this has but one end: Jewish supremacy over the Aryan and, subsequently, the planet. The threat of "baby-killing brutes" always appears when the Jew is near. Nietzsche understood this point better than most:

> When Jews step forward as the personification of innocence, the danger must be great…. [T]he Jews: an instinctively crafty people, able to create an advantage, a means of *seduction* out of every conceivable hypothesis of superstition, even out of ignorance itself.[20]

Ignorance — we are all meant to ignore the fact that Judeo-Christianity used absolute brutality to convert Nature-oriented Aryans to Judeo-subservience, that crusades benefited only the wealthy (i.e., the Jews and their "elite" Christian puppets), that the Jews slaughtered millions of Aryans in the Russian Revolution and its consequent *red terrors* and *deracinations* the world over, that the Jews orchestrated two world wars for their collective profit,[21] and that the Jews have stolen Palestinian land and pummeled the Palestinian people with the help of their Judeo-Allies (Britain, the United States, and, increasingly, all of Europe). Perhaps future technology will exist allowing for a Lord Balfour, Churchill, or Roosevelt to be resurrected and we can ask them about their debts to the Jews, or what they really gained from their Judeo-pacts.

Of course, these questions will never be asked in a fantastical future nor in our present situation — because the whole "technological" system is gripped by the Jew. One is never allowed to question the Jews or their means; to do so would only be "anti-Semitic." And if facts themselves are not anti-Semitic, then the facts must simply be *changed* to favor the Jew — *for all time*, as the Jews are wont to do.

This of course is the real reason for the existence of the Judeo-system: to mask the Jews' domination of the modern world. This "instinctively crafty people ... create an advantage" out of being the doormat of history: no one has or ever will play the victim better than the "hapless" Jew. *It is all forgery*: no people are as zealous, spiteful, depraved, violent, and scheming as Jews. The "crafty people" create the self-serving "facts" necessary to subjugate the world. "We own the science," says the Jew — and why not? They own everything else. Aren't they, after all, the *most intelligent* of all the races?

The Jews would have us all believe they use their canny intelligence to benefit humanity and *never* to manipulate the masses for their own profit. This, of course, is why so many Jews end up in finance (*economics*), technology (*mechanization*), media, medicine, academia, and government/law (*indoctrination* and *legislation*) — it's because they were forced into such roles! Yes, of course! Jews would be simple *farmers* and *miners* and *laborers* — if only the wicked Aryan would stop forcing them into positions of power and influence over the masses they are so eager to "help." Perhaps Menasseh ben Israel was mistaken in his letter to Oliver Cromwell:

> It is a thing confirmed, that merchandizing is, as it were, the proper profession of the Nation of the Jews... God ... hath given his people, as it were, a natural instinct, by which they might not only gain what is necessary for their need, but that they should also thrive in Riches and possessions, whereby they should not only become gracious to their Princes and Lords, but

that they should be invited by others to come and dwell in their Lands.²²

Yes, perhaps he was mistaken. Jews were only minding their innocent business in Germany, Russia, England, Spain, France, Italy, Egypt, Algeria, Hungary, Austria, and elsewhere — when, *all of a sudden*, they were inexplicably expelled. Those wicked Gentiles — always harassing the innocent Jew!

The poor, luckless Jew — it hides its scheming well in the shadows. And the longer the Jewish covenant with the Lord of Darkness can be concealed, the more time is bought to run roughshod over creation before the bitter end: Satan-Jehovah and its golems exist solely to sully existence, after all. Who can look seriously at the television's talking heads and nod in agreement at the Jew- and Israel-loving nonsense being spewed? Actually, many people — *most*, in fact. And the materialists believe in the possibility of a political solution! The real solution rests in the dissolution of the system that supposes a political solution is imaginable.

3.

Population is the mass. The mass is the dreck. Duped, drugged, and somnambulant, the dreck must be culled. Naturally, the dreck virulently oppose such culling; besides their moments of unconditional support for Israel and effeminate allegiance to the athletes they worship on a weekly basis, this particular subject is perhaps most dear to them. *Leave me my Israel, my sports, and my life*: such is the mantra of the masses. "The crowd's way is always broad," wrote Kierkegaard. "There the poisonous ornamental flower of excuses is found in bloom.... This way leadeth not unto life."²³ Israel exists for the Jews; sport is distraction; your life is a tool for Jewish supremacy. That the dreck fail to see how each of their deepest desires is related speaks to their obliviousness. Not to worry: the dreck will never awaken to their existence as fodder for the Judeo-system. No amount of "metapolitical" persuasion will convince the inconvincible. (But never forget that those seeking *political* solution care little for actual solutions; their goal is material gain and power.)

We have surpassed eight billion people on this earth. We are expected to believe, simultaneously, according to those who stand to gain the most from propping up the Judeo-system, that (1) we have an overpopulation problem and (2) each life has value. This is a dissonance that cannot be reconciled. If we have an overpopulation problem, not every life can have value, despite the lip service paid to such a notion. Likewise, if every life has value, we cannot have an overpopulation problem.

Hitlerists wholly reject the notion that each life has value; *value is earned*. Who defines value? It is always the strongest who define value — not necessarily in terms of quality, but quantity too. The Hitlerist, who is not now nor ever will be the strongest quantitatively, sees Nature as qualitatively strongest and therefore uses Nature to define value. "The bungled and the botched"[24] should be discarded, for they are against Nature. Who decides what counts as "bungled and botched"? Let Nature decide. Nietzsche assesses our current situation:

> ... *Anti-Nature* ascended the throne. With relentless logic the last step was reached, and this was the absolute demand to *deny Nature*....
>
> What the species requires is the suppression of the physiologically botched, the weak and the degenerate: but it was precisely to these people that Christianity appealed as a *preservative* force, it simply strengthened that natural and very strong instinct of all the weak which bids them protect, maintain, and mutually support each other. What is Christian "virtue" and "love of men," if not precisely this mutual assistance with a view to survival, this solidarity of the weak, this thwarting of selection? What is Christian altruism, if it is not the mob-egotism of the weak which divines that, if everybody looks after everybody else, every individual will be preserved for a longer period of time? ... He who does not consider this attitude of mind as *immoral*, as a crime against life, himself belongs to the sickly crowd, and also shares their instincts...[25]

2 — Population and Technics

Stop running from subjectivity, coward! Reason (or as Nietzsche says above, *logic*), in the hands of the Jew, is nothing more than indoctrinatory dogma; it is the artifice of "objectivity" meant to obscure evaluative motives.[26] Is this what you care to use to determine health and strength? What constitutes the Jew's "reason"? *What is good for the Jew*, of course! Modern notions of "objectivity" have their source in *Jewish subjectivity*, i.e., Jewish valuations. Before the so-called Enlightenment, European man was mesmerized with Judeo-Christianity. Beginning with the Enlightenment, this enthrallment simply changed hands to secularism, or humanism, or — *liberalism*. Whatever one wishes to call it — today it might be called *globalism* — it was *rationality*, reason over *all*. "Reason" and "objectivity" are religiously and zealously pushed because this is a principal way to dupe the masses. "We own the science" — indeed they do. Recall the UN Under-Secretary; she extolled her fellow Jews welcoming refugees. Think of the porous borders: porous borders *only ever work in one direction*: to dilute the European populations.

Porous borders, refugee asylum, and mass immigration, generally, are typically justified with an *economics*-based argument: migrants must be moved into historically-European lands because of the guaranteed *economic* dividends *new perspectives* bring and because native European populations are *declining anyway*; *someone* needs to fill anticipated vacancies, so it might as well be the *fecund* non-Europeans who *pick up the slack*.[27] Why European populations are declining deserves its own full study, but two important factors might be (1) the demoralization of European peoples through two Jew-driven world wars and more than a century of expeditionary, imperialistic conflict, and (2) the pivot from traditional, *Aryan* lifeways to modern, *Judeo* norms that prioritize money, materialism, and the dissolution of family. Spengler realized that Aryan lifeways are

> conservative ... and [grow] out of whatever fundamental life-forces still exist in Nordic peoples: instinct for power and possessions; for possessions *as* power; for inheritance, fecundity, and family, which three belong

together; for distinctions of rank and social gradation, whose mortal enemy was (or is) Rationalism from 1750 to 1950.²⁸

The rise of the non-European weed uproots the Aryan and hinders his resistance to the Jews' imposed and spiritually void existence. Serrano rightly observes a distinction between *Imperium* and *imperialism*: "That of [Aryan] Rome was Imperium; that of England, imperialism."²⁹ Imperium advances spiritual-cultural race, which is *freedom*; imperialism advances *servitude*, or economics and mechanization — the dehumanization of man for material gain. Jewish *Imperium* is really Jewish *imperialism*. The soulless golem, in the image of its Demiurge-fabricator, has no other interest than materiality and its continued manufacture — for this constitutes a revolt against Nature and the Supreme Creator. *Insurgency by existence*: this is the nature of the Jew.

> The privilege of creation has been wrested from Nature.... Man has stepped outside the bounds of Nature, and with every fresh creation he departs further and further from her, becomes more and more her enemy. *That* is his "world history," the history of a steadily increasing, fateful rift between man's world and the universe...
>
> This is the beginning of man's *tragedy* — for Nature is the stronger of the two. Man remains dependent on her, for in spite of everything she embraces him, like all else, within herself. All the great Cultures are *defeats*. Whole races remain, inwardly destroyed and broken, fallen into barrenness and spiritual decay, as corpses on the field. The fight against Nature is hopeless and yet — it will be fought out to the bitter end.³⁰

Spengler, despite his brilliance, never saw the inimical Innocent Jew; he saw only Schopenhauerian cultural urges enacted on the historical stage. That is, there is not merely *rift* between the folks of this world, there is *blind rift*: folk fulfill their cultural destiny without reference to the cosmic motivations behind them. Spengler, of course, was no Hitlerist; for Spengler did not see God even when he looked in the mirror, let alone when he intuited the life of peoples. Thus he could not distinguish between "man" and "Jew" and each one's particular use of technics. Folks are not compartmentalized in the medium of history; they live, fight, and die for a *cosmic motivation* that transcends world history as a mere "potent ... form of the waking consciousness."[31] Without such cosmic motivation, there would be no culture. *Cosmic motivation* is the drive for Imperium, to impress upon *being itself*, and not just history, one's vision of God. Spirit-culture — i.e., *race* — is the drive to create a divine kingdom on earth.

This is why when cosmic impulses are replaced with material ones we are left with only a Jewish Imperium, a Judeo-system that recognizes neither God nor a Spenglerian-cyclical history.[32] It is the Jew that seeks to demolish Aryan lifeways and spirituality; it is the Jew that seeks to debase and mechanize man; it is the Jew that values money and the influence it carries above all. The "man-animal" and its "mechanical science" are "alone in the Universe."[33] There is nothing divine about one who senses divinity in a satanic soma, which is to say, one who irreverently discards God altogether. Jewish *Imperium* can only be Jewish *imperialism* — because *the Jew has no spiritual-cultural mandate to bring God to earth*; the Jew, at best, *is* god ("the Chosen"); at worst, the Jew imposes the enslaving will of its Satan-Jehovah on mankind.

But here is the secret: these scenarios — *Jew as god* and *Jew as emissary* — are not different. Why do porous borders work in only one direction? Because without the Aryan as obstacle, the Jew will more easily have its Imperium. This Imperium of the Anti-Race is a war against Nature; this Imperium of the Soulless is a war against Salvation — *for all time*. The Jew and its Judeo-system are usurpations of the cosmic current carrying man to the godly Idea, to communion with God. What we are instead left with is man "dehumanized and degraded into an animal by the force of economic necessity."[34] *Man as commodity*: this is the Jewish Imperium.

The Organization for Economic Cooperation and Development (OECD) is one of the leading influences behind the commoditization of man, behind the notion of "migrants as investments." It annually produces roughly a thousand publications "spanning public policy." Formed out of the ashes of World War II, the OECD is comprised almost exclusively of European countries or countries that are of mainly European stock.[35] These countries have "an obligation" to help, in essence, nonwhite countries; one form of help is the acceptance and support of migrants. What became the OECD was first led by the Marxist Robert Marjolin (OEEC Secretary General, 1948-1955); this reflected the tenor of the organization and its goals. Member nations of the OECD are assessed annually in the Commitment to Development Index "on their dedication to policies that benefit the five billion people living in poorer nations"; the current top-ten ranking countries are Sweden, Germany, Norway, Finland, France, Netherlands, the UK, Switzerland, Austria, and Canada — all are countries with diplomatic and assistance ties to Israel; all are countries, save for Finland, with Holocaust memorials[36]; all are countries accepting throngs of nonwhite immigrants, diluting native European populations.

Doctors Henry Garrett, Richard Lynn, John R. Baker, Charles Murray, James Watson, and many others have noted the unequivocal correlation between race and intelligence.[37] What comes to them? They are maligned as "conspiracy theorists" or "kooks," apparently "bending" or "falsifying" statistics to fit their worldview: All Jewry — to include the Judaized Gentiles — pushes this narrative until it is a powerful slogan rattling the masses' neurons to reactivity.[38] Science and statistics are "false" or "misleading" when their conclusions differ from those of the Judeo-system. Thus the world abounds with "conspiracies," "canards," and "tropes" — especially those of the "anti-Semitic" and "racist" variety. Words are weaponized to silence dissenters.

Nevertheless, a trope repeated: If the "Great Replacement" is *not* real (which it is), the completely innocent and apparently naïve political system is missing an incredible opportunity. *Why wouldn't you*, as an unscrupulous leftist politician hoping to maintain power for as long as humanly possible, welcome non-native voters to dilute both the intelligence and the "conservative" values of your population? *Why wouldn't you* give these potential voters a free

2 — Population and Technics 73

pass on nearly everything, and *why wouldn't you* give these potential voters free handouts at every turn in an attempt to win their future support? Of course you would; and of course they do. What pundit and talking head hasn't orgasmically lauded the demise of the "white voter," the "white population"? And if some "conservative" commentator has questioned the parade of analysts in favor of white demise, this same commentator will *always*, quite loyally to the system, immediately praise the very "important" immigration policy and the dire "need" for constant, but "controlled" immigration. And we are all supposed to believe the "liberals" and "conservatives" are not actually supporting the same agenda. It is all part of the Judeo-system.

The determining factor of what stays and goes, of what can be seen as "dreck" and what has value, is answer to the question, *What supports the Judeo-system?* That which supports the system must be eliminated; that which fights against the system — if it is healthy in mind, body, and spirit[39] — should be salvaged. Supporters of the Judeo-system wish nothing but death and damnation on Hitlerists and anyone working for the end of the wickedness harboring the wicked. They are, after all, part of a system "which bids them protect, maintain, and mutually support each other."[40] Nothing can be done about this; the evil never know they are evil; it is impossible to convince the duped, drugged, and dreaming that Jews constantly deceive and obfuscate for selfish gain; it is impossible to convince the dreck that their very being goes against divine Nature, that existing doesn't just mean slaving away in technological bondage for pittance and the pitiful reprieves distraction can offer; it is impossible to convince the population that *restricting* freedom will never amount to *more* freedom, let alone security, the opposite of which — *that less freedom equals more freedom and security* — the Jews and their collaborators are wont to emphasize.

The world is indeed overpopulated — with dreck. Beware of anyone who is *aghast* at the necessity of regulating the population, for they *are* the dreck. According to the dreck's wholly selfish nature, they will surely respond with, *If you're so concerned about overpopulation, why don't you start with yourself first?* Gladly: To the point of self-sacrifice does the Hitlerist act in his fight against cosmic unrighteousness. "Because," says Serrano, *"life is good for nothing if it is not sacrificed for an Ideal..."*[41] This is not "political" misstep, this is divine duty; it is the absolute duty to God that faith demands. Just know, dreck, that more than a few of you will be in tow.

Sacrifice is something the dreck will never comprehend — especially not with Israel, sport, and an exceedingly inconsequential existence ever on their hive-mind. One could argue that who lives and who dies should be contingent upon health, intelligence, or character — but, unhappily, none of these things matter anymore. We are in the Kali-Yuga, and anything of significance matters less and less each passing day. Everything today

> is a product of ... modern "objective science..." [Drugs, for instance,] are designed to extend physical life, but they do not cause man to find himself, nor to be more wise, nor to reach divinity, nor his totality. For that is not the intended [purpose]. On the contrary, they will continue to denigrate ... and materialize man more and more, so that men can arrive at being a sort of living-dead, a living corpse perhaps two hundred years old, a Zombie![42]

They are the keepers of the Judeo-system, and *they* want legions of drones, or "zombies," to feed the Lord of Darkness perpetuating it; constant crises, endless Judeo-wars, societal-correctness — all such specters of the senses contribute to the fevered potion that feeds the Organic Lie, the Breathing Hate, the satanic Jehovah. Already in 1993 Serrano deplored the coming onslaught of "parodies of real [men]" — because the youth had simply become "ignorant muses and drug addicts."[43] This fact has only been exacerbated for us in the era of the Duped, Drugged, and Dreaming.

Make no mistake: those destined to be valueless will ever be without value, just as those destined for honor, discipline, and integrity will have it *nonetheless*. "Some men are called *sons of hell*, not as being born of hell, but as prepared for it, as the *sons of the kingdom* are prepared for the kingdom."[44] That is, if one falls from the path, one was never on the path and never would have been;

there is only success or failure in this existential combat of the Cosmic Struggle. Those who "don't make it" were lost from the beginning, and they are never worth another's time. If another "makes it" along the true path, this one would have made it regardless of another's intervention. In short, *help those only willing and able to help themselves*; no one else is viable.⁴⁵

4.

Joseph Goebbels grasped the situation well: "There is only one solution: to deal radically with the danger."⁴⁶ Do you understand? It cannot be said more clearly. What is the danger? Adolf Hitler has unmasked the Jew *for all time*: at best, the Aryan people will be exterminated; at worst, they will be enslaved. Yes, those who become slaves to a system that hates them deserve to be enslaved. We recall Kierkegaard: *It is great to deserve the tears of those who deserve to shed tears.*⁴⁷ This is meant here in its most scornful sense. Yet in this darkest of ages, even those who deserve to shed tears are either too heedless or too spiteful to weep — especially, in their eternal contempt, are they unable to weep for the quality around them, which serves as constant reminder of their inferiority.

> And this do I say also to the o'erthrowers of statues: It is certainly the greatest folly to throw salt into the sea, and statues into the mud. In the mud of your contempt lay the statue: but it is just its law, that out of contempt, its life and living beauty grow again!⁴⁸

We make no promises for Nietzsche here. Let the contempt of the quantity swell. The time for rebirth is past; Shiva hungers for the system; what follows in his wake happens regardless of yesterday's pledges. Contempt stifles tears; the Judeo-bots can keep their tears for the manufactured crises the Jews regularly dangle before them, however; that we fighters against the Judeo-system act so as to deserve the wretched weeping of the Judaized dreck is sufficient.

"Extreme positions are not relieved by more moderate ones, but by extreme *opposite* positions," wrote Nietzsche.⁴⁹ There is no precedent for the fanaticism the near future will witness. The Jews have pressed the world into a corner with their boundless contempt for all life. Their hatred is powerful. However — life, too, is powerful. Those who negate will, in turn, be negated.

Hitler, too, speaks: "Compulsion can only be broken through compulsion, and terror only by terror. Only then can a new order be created."[50] One cannot set sights on a "new order" until the Judeo-system is finished. A "new order" will come of its own accord, and it will come long after our time is gone. Let the politically minded materialists who unwittingly work for the Jew obsess over the post-fanatical world; they are blind to the present responsibility. The task for those living now is *fanaticism* — it is the destruction of the Judeo-system. The Aryan must "*destroy the hypnosis paralyzing men and women of our own physical and spiritual race ... with ... ancient fury.*"[51] A Fury stands behind the Jew. What will you command it do?

> [The galvanization of the] masses ... can only happen by ruthlessly and fanatically concentrating on achieving a one-sided goal.... [A people can only be electrified] with the intensity that comes from taking an extreme position. Poison is driven out only by counter-poison...[52]

Thus wrote Hitler in *Mein Kampf*. The poisonous mushroom has festered in the dark for long enough. To rid the soil of the *ferment of decomposition*, care must be taken to dry the soil, to bring light to the soil, to expose the soil to fresh and vibrant air. Killing the poison mushroom without *fundamentally altering the conditions that spawn it* is wasted effort. Change the conditions and the mushroom will die without further intervention. A new wind shifts the stagnant air, bending it around the festering fungus; a fiery sun rides the wind, and its warmth is the whirling Fury branding a destiny as old as time.

5.

What is population?

Population is the *tamasic* mass, heated to a molten dollop and forged by *rajasic* cadres into a drab, dense wave that breaks over

Nature and her upholders. Population is a tool in the hands of the Enemy, which is why it will increase in this Kali-Yuga. Population is a demiurgic cancer molded by the mind of the Jew. Population is the Organic Weapon in the hand of the Organic Lie.

Population — is technics.

Technics

According to Spengler, "*Technics is the tactics of life*; it is the inner form of which the *process* of conflict — identical with life itself — is the outward expression." What matters is not the tool, but the process of using the tool: "not the weapon, but the battle."[53] The battle is born of the combatants, whose natures set the conditions of conflict; the weapons used are determined by the nature of the struggle. The weapons and the battle share their essence with the character of the combatant, and one is not divisible from the other.

Life and the tools one uses to navigate it flow from the inward drive of those destined to confront it. The inward drive of the Aryan is creation; the inward drive of the Jew is destruction. Each combatant fulfills its role in the Cosmic Struggle, whose purpose can only be divined when one breaks from understanding through the leap of faith.[54] The leap of faith is exclusively the domain of creativity and, therefore, the Aryan. The destructive urge of rationalistic materialism, on the other hand, is dominion of the Jew.

Spengler saw that technology was something godlike:

> With the coming of rationalism, the belief in technics almost becomes a materialistic religion. Technics is eternal and immortal like God the Father, it delivers mankind like God the Son, and it illumines us like God the Holy Ghost. And its worshipper is the progress-philistine of the modern age...[55]

There is no "*almost* becomes a materialistic religion" — this rationalism, or *scientism*, is the unquestionable ideology, or *religion*, of the current world movers who use internationalism, or *globalism*, to further their material ambitions. Science as a tool to augment an understanding of the material world, to complement the spiritual, *does not exist*; instead, what we have is the monolithic SCIENCE — no longer a mere tool, but an elevated, satanic subterfuge, a dogmatic deception meant to subjugate the herd. According to Serrano,

> [Judeo-scientism] has made itself into a new absolutism in order to impose and apply to any past or future contingency ("Before me, *nothing*; after me, *less*"). It is a new dogma, a "science of Marxism," a "physics of Freudianism." Jew myth and mysticism.[56]

Leading the charge as primary *combatant* for godless materialism is the Jew; the *battle* it wages is against Nature and her defenders: The Jew means to "enslave and harness [Nature's] very forces so as to multiply [its] own strength."[57] There is nothing harmonious about this, but only a heavy-handed effort to pummel resistance into the proper mold, the proper weapon. The *weapon* is the mass, the population. The population is weaponized through the propaganda identified by both *Jew* ("manipulation of the ... habits and opinions of the masses is an important element in democratic society") and *dissenter* ("the system ... must exert constant pressure on people to mold their behavior").[58] What we are left with — what we are *confronted* with — is *a globalist religion of scientism led from the shadows by the high priests of demiurgical materialism*: the Jews.

The "progress-philistine of the modern age," the proto-zombie, the Judeo-bot, is the weaponized population agitating on behalf of the Jews and their enrichment; the weaponization occurs because of the masses' manufactured desire to enjoy some scraps spilling from the altar to Satan-Jehovah.

That the Jew uses the population as a weapon is telling: Jews see the masses as a tool to be employed for their benefit.[59] This aligns with Jewish sentiment and doctrine that non-Jews are simply cattle for herding in this or that Jew-serving direction. It also accords with their instinct to remain hidden among the herd; the more (spiritual-cultural) turbidity among the people, the more comfort for the Jew — there is harbor in havoc: not only can situations be exploited for gain (e.g., war profiteering, money laundering, political jockeying), but the masses in such situations become more susceptible to manipulation (i.e., through the proven method of *divide and conquer*). With sociopolitical chaos, it takes little effort to mask oneself behind an ancestral name change here, a Gentile frontman there.

Because the masses are naught but weapon for the Jews, the latter feel no connection with the former. This aligns with their long history of being a people apart — i.e., a society within (or without) a society, an anti-race who "maintained their internal solidarity."[60] Yet the weapons and the battle share their essence with the character of the combatant — in this case, the Jew. How can the Jew remain apart from, yet share an essence with the masses? The essence of the Jew is *destruction* — the international parasite cannot help but destroy native Aryan cultures and incessantly press for war and bloodletting. The Gentile masses do not have this innate bloodlust, but their *profound* ignorance and credulity make them pliant in the hands of skilled craftsmen.

The masses' *will* becomes one with the Jews' through propaganda, to be sure, but the Jew remains distinct through its intense disdain for the people upon which it preys. For the Jew is the *master* of the population it both wields and needs to sustain its death-ride into the unholy bosom of Satan-Jehovah. Jews loathe the masses they manipulate — for Jews are the Organic Lie, the Breathing Hate. This hatred, which manifests as meddlesome materialism, is born of their father, the Lord of Darkness, whose single purpose is to play *nemesis* to Nature, to the Supreme Creator. This is why the all-too-common *Jewish philanthropy* is oxymoronic: Jews could never love (*philo*) the people (*anthropo*) they purport to help — they are the supreme *misanthropes*, and their "help" for others is *always* only profit for themselves.

This is why the Jew is the vessel of anti-blood and pits its entire being against the natural laws of blood (race) and soil (earth). Nature, for the Jew, exists to be exploited and destroyed. The manufactured masses are in lockstep with their master, and all now serve the Lord of Darkness; thus, advancing either the masses or their master is satanic.

The shared essence of the Jew and its weaponized herd of Gentiles is only another reason to end the Judeo-system. They are distinct by blood, but not spirit; and their anti-spirit perpetuates and feeds on the system. End the system and you end their vile spirit.

6.

What few Aryans remain still uphold creation and creativity. Their battle is and was against the weighty forces constraining their lofty spirit; their weapons were towering spires, ethereal art, ingenious engineering, and venturous expeditions. Aryans sought to conquer and beautify the world because they felt the tug of their divine ancestors; by reaching for the heavens, they could edge just a little closer to God. "To build a world *oneself*, to be *oneself* God — that is the Faustian inventor's dream, and from it has sprung all our designing and redesigning of machines to approximate as nearly as possible to the unattainable limit of perpetual motion."[61] What is this *perpetual motion* if not the seemingly unattainable, if not God? From the beginning, Aryans have used the power of Nature to revere her: fashion the tool, conquer the foe, erect the monument, honor the gods. It is the monument itself that stands as the decisive implement, for it expresses the ultimate Aryan vision — it is the inward drive of the *strong man in victory*,[62] it is the revelation of a man discovering himself.

With such ambitions, the Aryan cannot but combat the Jew, Golem of the Ghastly, Demon of the Demiurge. The Jew is the beast to the Aryan beauty. Beasts are meant to be bested, however; and the coming Siegfried seeks no treasure beyond the pleasure of ending a foul fiend — *that* is the real beauty. Thus writes Serrano:

> Everything these *Golem* attempt to make the world forget Adolf Hitler and his comrade Rudolf Hess ... will not have the desired effect, even going so far as to use hypnotic influences on the masses. Esoteric Hitlerism ... will prevail, helped by the very things the *Golem* do to fight against it. Jehovah and his *Golem* will annihilate each other within their automatized Universe, together with the society of ants they foster. That will be the end of *Kali Yuga*.[63]

What role can the Aryan play in such a self-destructive drama? It is clear: The Aryan is here to represent the Divine on earth; the Aryan is a steward for God — for decency and discipline, for honor and loyalty. *Meine Ehre heißt Treue!* The Aryan's role in this self-destructive drama is to be *creative*, to *love* the good, and to be *absolutely unmerciful* toward evil. The Aryan is the opposite of the Jew. "[Destruction of the world] is the labor of the Jew and his Archetype, the Lord of Chaos and Darkness. The Jew cannot do otherwise, he has been programmed for this labor."[64]

Using the masses as its desired weapon in the Cosmic Struggle, the Jew aims to both *technicize* the Aryan and overwhelm him with sheer *numbers*. The purpose is to imprison the Aryan within the Judeo-system, to overwrite his soul with the assembly-line stamp, thus attempting to erase all memory of the Supreme Creator in Jehovah's crass imitation. But the Aryan's "Faustian technics are in no wise an inward necessity. *It is only Faustian man* that thinks, feels, and *lives* in this form. To him it is a *spiritual* need, not on account of its economic consequences, but on account of its *victories*."[65] That is, the Aryan remains *free* — *free* because he is driven by that which transcends. Triumphantly, then, the memory of God cannot be erased. The Jew is compelled by its inner drive to destruction, however, and so enlists the colored horde to quell the memory.

"For the colored races, on the contrary, [the Aryan implement] is but a weapon in their fight against the Faustian civilization, a weapon like a tree from the woods that one uses as house-timber, but discards as soon as it has served its purpose."[66] This secret, which will forever remain a secret to the sightless Jew, is the ticking time bomb that promises final Jewish destruction: the Jew hates the Aryan and wants him dead; the Jew sees with sightless eyes that it needs the Aryan to perpetuate the Judeo-system, so it pursues enslavement instead; Aryan enslavement means reliance upon nonwhites for perpetuating the system; Aryan fanaticism means ever decreasing participation in and ever increasing fighting against the system; the Jew therefore opens Pandora's Box through its increased employment of animal-men — though it is no box, but only the thresher-jaws of Satan-Jehovah.

The Jew will certainly destroy this world — and Hitlerist accelerationists will help. It is just as well. Would you imagine the birth of a post-apocalyptic Golden Age wherein all is right with the world? A fantastical racial paradise? *Nonsense!* This is not mere impossibility — this is blasphemy! Or does one suppose the will of God could be outdone? The time for racial paradise ended — *for all time* — with *Götterdämmerung* in 1945. And even then, such an outcome was not fated and, therefore, *impossible*. Can you imagine now some new, post-apocalyptic racial paradise that *wouldn't* be betrayed by the dreck — by the Fenrirs-in-fleece *ethnocentrists*, by the money-minded *Straßers*, by the Judeo-Christian *Banhöffers*? Is the rebuilding of *society* (that euphemism for *cancer*) even fathomable if, as must happen, the mass of *humans* (that euphemism for *cancer cells*) is eradicated? Should we pursue a resurrection of the rotted flesh?

It is amusing when Veryan Khan, president and CEO of the Terrorism Research and Analysis Consortium, warns the world, "[The accelerationists'] main goal is to collapse society so they can rebuild it for the white man"[67] — the "white man," like every other *cancer cell* on this earth, is a *falsified husk*, branded with the sign and seal of *Jehovah*, whether his language is Liberalism, Marxism, Judeo-Christianity, Ethnocentrism, Atheism, Capitalism, Globalism, Humanism, or even jackbooting *Nazism*. They are all *materialists* seeking *materialistic power*, and they are all acolytes of Satan, the Lord of Shadows. What is the difference between Veryan Khan, who so woefully misunderstands[68] the "accelerationist" mission, and, say, our modern "ethnocentrists"? Perhaps only melanin — for their branded souls are the same; they are all just food for the Demiurge.

> *Out of the sludgy mortar new offspring*
> *Formed like men.*
> *These hybrids were deaf*
> *To the intelligence of heaven. They were revolted*
> *By the very idea*
> *Of a god...*

> *Now comes the love of gain — a new god.*
> *Made out of the shadow...*
>
> *Precious ores the Creator had concealed*
> *As close to hell as possible*
> *Were dug up — a new drug*
> *For the criminal.*[69]

The fodder, in turn, feeds itself on the ores extracted from the stones and mountains plugging the abyss. The *Steins, Sterns, Bergs, Mans*, those who remain hidden behind the *Ur-Mann* and *Ur-Manu*, and all those hoping to engorge themselves on the scraps are sated only by the criminality their lust for material gain imposes upon Nature. For theirs is the god that deceives, theirs is the god that kills; theirs is the god that terror conceives and fills with terrible ills.

7.

From whence does the Demiurge come?

At the dawn of nonexistent time, when harmony turned to maelstrom, Kronos felt a pang in his gut that could never be called *hunger* by any human measure; it was instead a life-retarding emptiness he begged desperately to subdue. And whom did he beg but the hate that drove the figurative to figures? Kronos' emptiness was a lust for power, and from this unnatural envy came the unwholesome entreaties of his mal-fashioned mother: *Harm your father, Kronos; your time has come!* Father of Linear Time, Kronos, played nemesis to his Creator, and this became the spirit of unnatural rebellion that still thrives in his linear-minded lackeys. From his dishonorable and disloyal hand sprung the sickle! *The sickle!* — His *hammer* was the hardened, hate-filled hole within him.

So Kronos ambushed his father and castrated him. Kronos filled his pit with a foul deed, but his hate was unsatiated: his children, he was promised, would rise up against him just as he rebelled against his father. To thwart this prophecy, fell Kronos devoured his children. One can see similarities between Kronos' misdeeds and Jacob's — Jacob, the *golem* who became *Israel*: the conniving mother deceives the father to elevate the wicked son to power.⁷⁰ The stories share an author: the Craftsman, Demiurge-Jehovah. It is indeed true that the author can author *his* own *story* — such is the *history* of the Jew. And the Jew's attempt to erase the figurative nature of time with linearity is an attempt to erase its own foul origins. Kronos' technics were hammer and sickle; the Jews' hammer and sickle is population. The population reaps the Jews' world-destroying will.

Kronos has another name: Saturn. Saturn's day is Saturday — the Jewish Sabbath. Jews honor their satanic father on the Sabbath and enjoy practicing their mastery over slaves on their unholy day; they do this by employing Gentiles to run errands for them. Jews call their gofers *shabbos-goyim* — *Sabbath Cattle*. We remember that Kronos did not retain supremacy: he was deposed and defeated by his sixth child, Zeus. Zeus, god of sky, god of lightning — Thor, god of thunder — Wotan, god of sky, god of lightning — *Blitzkrieg* is Lightning War, Wotan's War. *Zeus, the sixth child*: The memory of Kronos' defeat by the Aryan Zeus has never left the Jews and their Lord of Darkness. Six — 6 — is the ritualistic number of the Jews because it serves as a reminder of their ignominy: they use it now to shame their ultimate foe, the Aryan — *for all time*.⁷¹

The masses are immured in their Pavlovian response to the *Six Million*, to *D-Day* — the 6th hour on the 6th day of the 6th month —, to the *Six-Pointed Star* (Magen David), to the *Six Days of Creation*, to the *Sabbath of the Sixth ("Seventh") Day* (Saturn's Day), to the *Six Books of the Oral Torah* (the Mishnah), and so on. Always the Jew elicits an emotional response from its molded masses. Thinking is for the Jew, not for you. Population — the tool — obliges.

8.

Technics today are only the absence of fanaticism and our approach toward the hive-mind. The future is a rebellion against the technics the Jews use to mechanize the masses and subsequently mold them into the ultimate organic implement. Thus, the future is *fanatical*.

Where one formerly used a fist, one now fires the bullet. How much more fanatical, how much more enraged must a man be to engage in hand-to-hand combat with his enemy than to simply squeeze a trigger — *How easy it is for the Jews to slaughter 15,000*

Palestinians in Gaza with bombs and bullets! How easy it is for Israel to provide "indefinite security" in Gaza with the omnipresent threat of technicized violence! — The point is illustrated beyond just violence, however. Where one once crafted food or shelter with staid hands, sure eyes, and a dogged determination, one now buys readymade products. Where one walked endless distances, braving elements or intrigue, for necessity or pleasure, one can now speed above the surface with minimal effort or discomfort. Technics stands in inverse ratio with fanaticism: as technics rise, so does fanaticism fall. This is not to impugn technics *qua* technics. It is, however, an observation and warning.

Sidewalks are saturated with organic drones basking in the cold glow of a screen. They are *freely in bondage* as they *fulfill with pleasure the will of their master*.[72] The hate-filled hole of Kronos swallows their minds' eyes. Serrano reminds us that

> [Aryans have] an additional nerve bundle enabling them to re-identify with the world of Divinity.... This [organ] is not found in colored races and allows the Aryan to see reality in a divine projection and perspective.... This marks a fundamental difference between the races, helping us to understand the meaning of the intention to hybridize the white peoples, carried out ... with growing intensity since 1945....[73]

Aryans are *de-Aryanized* — *devolved* —, and thus enslaved, through miscegenation. Miscegenation is normalized through propaganda (or social-engineering efforts) — This is the practical interpretation of the countless media efforts to emasculate and criminalize "white" males to essentially justify "white" women mixing with nonwhite (usually black) males; it is the practical interpretation of the relentless race mixing one sees in the media, generally, and the incessant elevation of nonwhite (almost always black) culture. In fact, however, *no Aryan has ever been hybridized*: no real Aryan would ever do such a thing; and such attempts to devolve the strong are only a preying on the weak. Nevertheless, the propaganda efforts continue — but these only hone the Aryan into the divine vessel destined for the final conflagration. The illuminated faces held captive by glowing prisons never were Aryan and never will be.

The Aryan's honor is loyalty.

9.

The most striking contrast to the Aryan is the Jew. There is probably no other people in the world who have so developed the instinct of self-preservation as the so-called chosen people. The best proof of this is the simple fact that this race still exists. Where are another people that, in the course of the last 2,000 years, have undergone so few changes in mental outlook and character as the Jews? What other people has been involved in greater revolutionary changes — and yet, even after the most gigantic catastrophes, has emerged unchanged? What an infinitely tenacious will-to-live, to preserve one's kind, is shown by that fact![74]

So writes Hitler in *Mein Kampf*. The Jew has been tailor-made to be the Prince of this World under the Lord of Darkness. This is the world we face. *No one* has ever defeated the Jew because everyone tries to defeat the Jew at its own game. It is instead essential that we attack and destroy the system itself — and stop trying to defeat the Jew *within* the system. *The days of politics are over*. Our time can only be defined by the complete eradication of the Judeo-system, and it can only resonate with Nature after a final solution to the Jewish problem. The Jew cannot be defeated at its own deceptive game. Aryan, you must tackle the system; destroy the system, and the Jew will follow.

Nothing to lose and everything to gain — this is the potent elixir, the danger beneath and within. Daily the danger grows for the Jew; its system is predicated on the *few Jews* obsessively accumulating benefit at the expense of the herd. The Jew cannot stop itself, nor can it stop the danger gathering against it; it has a destiny to fulfill — a destiny that will end in global catastrophe. Nothing will be lost in this catastrophe. Should we mourn the loss of dreck who so willingly serve the will of their master? The dreck will fall with the system they worship and slave to protect, just like their master. The Aryan stands in opposition to the Judeo-system, "from which its own creativeness has sundered it."[75] The Jewish Crusade aims to hammer all into submission with the two arms of its satanic cross: *fear* and *numbing*. The Jewish Crusade *will* dampen the creative spark it fears in Gentiles, and from this deadened ember will climb the smoky specter fated to haunt — not just Europe — but the whole godforsaken globe. This *is* destiny and it cannot be thwarted.

But for Spengler, the eternally creative Aryan harbors "the soul of a rebel,"[76] and the rebel, too, fulfills his destiny.

> Only dreamers believe in ways out. Optimism is *cowardice*. We are born into this time and must bravely follow the path to the destined end. There is no other way. Our duty is to hold on to the lost position, without hope, without rescue... *That* is greatness. *That* is what it means to have *race*. The *honorable end* is the *one thing* that cannot be taken from a man.[77]

Meine Ehre heißt Treue: Purity of heart is to will *one thing*.

Population and Technics — Notes

[1] Ernst Jünger, "Nationalist Revolution," *Die Standarte* (20 May 1926).
[2] Melissa Ruth Fleming, World Economic Forum, October 2022. Fleming, almost certainly a Jew herself, has hosted or participated in several pro-Jew events over the years, often decrying "hate speech" or "anti-Semitism."
[3] "The substance of the Enemy is the rational intelligence. One could therefore conclude that the rationalist thinking of the earthly is a demiurgic aggregate, a trap by means of which the Demiurge keeps them in chains. It is useless, therefore, to expect to overcome it using only the intellect. The effective weapon, the only one that the Demon fears, is the *Sieg* Rune, transcendent... The Thunderbolt with which Shiva destroys the Demon..." (Miguel Serrano, *Manu: For the Man to Come* [2017], 177).
[4] "How the Jewish community in Boston is welcoming Syrian refugees. Beautiful" (26 March 2017).
[5] *The View From Sunset Boulevard* (1979), 104.
[6] "To abandon oneself to expectations which are never fulfilled is to be reputed *progressive*" (Bruck, *Das Dritte Reich* [2012], 52).
[7] Stein, *The View From Sunset Boulevard*, 11, 13, 33-35, 38, 97, 106, respectively.
[8] *The View From Sunset Boulevard*, 136.
[9] *The Will to Power*, §2.
[10] Oswald Spengler, *The Decline of the West* (2006), 358.
[11] Miguel Serrano, *Hitler's UFO Against the New World Order* (2016), "The Speech," 21.
[12] Spengler, *The Hour of Decision* (2002), 87.
[13] *Industrial Society and Its Future*, paragraphs 114, 117, 119; emphasis added.
[14] Jeffrey Herf, *Reactionary Modernism: Technology, Culture, and Politics in Weimar and the Third Reich* (1990), 124; quoting Hans Freyer.
[15] Cf. chapter 1, fn88 above.
[16] Edward Bernays, *Propaganda* (2005 [originally published in 1928]), 48.
[17] First, *legality* and *rule of law* are masks tyrants hide behind as the snare tightens. Being masks, the Jew often finds work in law and government. *Rule of law* is a pillar of Judeo-democracy because its haughtiness hides backdoor deals, cronyism, and domestic and international criminality. *Rule of law* is an endlessly repeated *slogan* in liberal-democracies because such systems require the manipulation of public opinion to survive. The public is manipulated, in part, through slogan-

eering. "The conscious and intelligent manipulation of the organized habits and opinions of the masses is an important element in democratic society.... The important thing for the statesman of our age is not so much to know how to *please* the public, but to know how to *sway* the public" (Bernays, *Propaganda*, 37, 119).

Next, the Smith-Mundt Act (1948, the same year of the CIA's infiltration of mass media with Operation MOCKINGBIRD) in the United States, for example, restricts governmental communication with the citizenry. See "Private Ownership of Public Opinion" in *Myth and Sun: Essays of the ARCHETYPE* (2022) for more. We also often see the harmonious ideological marriage of a leftist *invisible* government and an increasingly leftist *overt* government manipulating public opinion through social media: there are always ways for "democratic" societies to circumvent the "laws" they have emplaced. The most recent glaring instance of this was the US (and other) government(s) and "Big Tech" cooperating to propagate various "we own the science"-type messages during the COVID-19 debacle/rights curtailment. However, ongoing, less conspicuous examples abound in the numerous proxy wars the US and its NATO partners wage and provoke across the globe.

[18] This is the perspective of the Zionist, the right-wing Jew. The Marxist, or left-wing Jew[†], perspective pretends to demonize Israel (or Zionism) in favor of, quite naturally, the dialectical-materialist approach; this approach is most clearly manifested today in globalism, which, unironically, envelops both the left and right of the Judeo-system. Globalism (and therefore denigration of Nature and Aryan) is the foundation for "diversity, equity, and inclusion" programs, corporate technocratization, and miscegenation; the purpose of these initiatives is to create a mongrelized race of drones united by a hive-mind in service of the Jew.

Globalism, which is to say *Jewry*, is behind both Zionism and Marxism. The dichotomy between "left-" and "right-wing" Jews is false — it is subterfuge meant only to further distract the masses, further fabricate the victimization of the Jew, and replenish broad sympathy for "The Chosen." The result of Zionism or Marxism is always the same: advance the cause of the Jew. If "left" and "right" posture as opponents, *all the better*, for it further confuses the masses, which has been Jewry's goal from the beginning. The Jew is the Demiurge's magician: it dazzles the eye with one hand and picks the pocket with the other; blood and treasure are funneled to Satan-Jehovah.

[†] *Marxist puppets* — the non-Jews who espouse Judeo-Marxism because of its violent, anti-Aryan character (e.g., in the US: Rashida Tlaib, Cori Bush, Summer Lee, Ayanna Pressley, Ilhan Omar, and countless

self-hating white and nonwhite "educators") — genuinely *do* despise Israel. This is because they mistakenly believe Jews are "white" and, quite simply, they *hate* all things European. More on this below (chapter 3, fn30). Moreover, from an economic standpoint, Marxists, as Spengler said, are only capitalists of the lower classes. *Hating whites and loving money*: this is the essence of Marxism.

[19] See Benton Bradberry's *The Myth of German Villainy*.
[20] Friedrich Nietzsche, *The Will to Power*, §199.
[21] Several sources exist to substantiate this, but a concise starting point is T. Dalton's *The Jewish Hand in the World Wars* (2019).
[22] From a 1655 plea to restore the Jews in England.
[23] Søren Kierkegaard, *Purity of Heart is to Will One Thing* (1956), 217.
[24] Nietzsche, *The Will to Power*, §55, §179, and elsewhere.
[25] Nietzsche, *The Will to Power*, §245 and §246.
[26] "All in all the time has come to put an end to the senseless ambition for objectivity which only leads to relativism and doubt in one's own strength. It is necessary to take a conscious one-sided position, giving priority to evaluation rather than 'understanding.'" Ernst Jünger, "The Frontline Soldier," *Die Standarte* (September 1925).
[27] See "Refugees are not a burden but an opportunity" and "Refugees Work: A humanitarian investment that yields economic dividends" (OECD; Legrain, 2016); "Refugees Are a Great Investment" (*Foreign Policy*; Legrain, 2017); "Refugees as Assets to Their New Countries" (International Monetary Fund, Edwards, 2022); "What are the Economic Benefits of Refugees?" (Lutheran Immigration and Refugee Service, 2022); "Refugees' Profound Economic Contributions" and "The Economic Impact of Refugees in America" (American Immigration Council, 2023); "Refugees Make America Better Off" (*Forbes*, Anderson, 2022); "Why accepting refugees is a win-win-win formula" (Brookings Institute, Bahar, 2018); "The Economic Impact of Refugees in America" (*Detroit Jewish News*, Fanek, 2023); "Refugees Are a Fiscal Success Story" (National Immigration Forum, 2018); "Refugees' Economic Contributions in the United States" and "Congress Must Reject Anti-Asylum Measures in Budget Proposals" (Hebrew Immigrant Aid Society, 2018 and 2023); etc.
[28] Spengler, *The Hour of Decision*, 194.
[29] *Resurrection of the Hero* (2015), 113.
[30] Oswald Spengler, *Man and Technics* (1963), 44-45. Some translations of this work have been modified to better match the original German.
[31] Spengler, *The Decline of the West*, 12.
[32] Spengler, *The Decline of the West*, 15.
[33] Serrano, *Adolf Hitler: The Ultimate Avatar* (2014), 323.

34 Howard L. Parsons, "The Prophetic Mission of Karl Marx," *The Journal of Religion* 44, no. 1 (1964), 53.
35 Japan is one of the few exceptions to this; it was "invited" into the OECD after the war† — because it exercised its cosmic, Imperium mandate. With the Shinto Directive and Potsdam Declaration, Japan surrendered its sovereignty and spiritual-cultural soul for material survival. As Clausewitz said, however, "the shame of a cowardly submission can never be erased. [T]his drop of poison in the blood of a folk is passed on to its descendants and will corrupt and undermine the strength of future generations" (*Political Testament*, 1812).

Japan's present emperor is biologically alive and enjoys playing the viola; he continues his father's tradition of not visiting the Yasukuni Shrine. Japan's people, meanwhile, are slowly dying — no doubt committing collective *hara-kiri* for not fulfilling their spiritual-cultural destiny.

† Japan became a *full* OECD member in 1964, devoting itself to achieving the organization's money-minded aims — *for all time.*
36 In April 2023, Switzerland's government approved funding for a memorial "to honor the six million Jews" (Keaten, AP, "Swiss to erect 1st national memorial honoring Nazi victims").
37 Garrett: *Children: Black & White* (1967) and *IQ and Racial Differences* (1980); Lynn: *Race Differences in Intelligence* (2015); Baker: *Race* (2016); Murray: *The Bell Curve* (1994); Watson, awarded the 1962 Nobel Prize in Physiology/Medicine, has made numerous remarks about the undeniable connection between race and intelligence stemming from his scientific discoveries, for which he has been repeatedly castigated and ostracized.

Regarding Watson, the National Library of Medicine, which falls under the United States Government's National Institutes of Health, surprisingly published Jason Malloy's "James Watson tells the inconvenient truth: faces the consequences" (April 2008); the full abstract is worth reproducing here:

> Recent comments by the eminent biologist James Watson concerning intelligence test data from sub-Saharan Africa resulted in professional sanctions as well as numerous public condemnations from the media and the scientific community. They justified these sanctions to the public through an abuse of trust, by suggesting that intelligence testing is a meaningless and discredited science, that there is no data to support Dr. Watson's comments, that genetic causes of group differences in intelligence are fal-

sified logically and empirically, and that such differences are already accounted for by known environment factors. None of these arguments are correct, much less beyond legitimate scientific debate. Dr. Watson was correct on all counts: (1) Intelligence tests do reveal large differences between European and sub-Saharan African nations, (2) the evidence does link these differences to universally valued outcomes, both within and between nations, and (3) there is data to suggest these differences are influenced by genetic factors. The media and the larger scientific community punished Dr. Watson for violating a social and political taboo, but fashioned their case to the public in terms of scientific ethics. This necessitated lying to the public about numerous scientific issues to make Watson appear negligent in his statements; a gross abuse of valuable and fragile public trust in scientific authority. Lies and a threatening, coercive atmosphere to free inquiry and exchange are damaging to science as an institution and to scientists as individuals, while voicing unfashionable hypotheses is not damaging to science. The ability to openly voice and argue ideas in good faith that are strange and frightening to some is, in fact, integral to science. Those that have participated in undermining this openness and fairness have therefore damaged science, even while claiming to protect it with the same behavior.

The aforementioned studies of race and intelligence indicate the *rule* and do not deal in absolutes. That is, there are, of course, intelligent and imbecilic members of every race, just as there are miscreants and examples of exceptional quality of every race. The studies measure capacities and capabilities of races as a whole, and in this measure there exist obvious disparities among the folk of this world.

38 Some "conservatives" (Jews or otherwise), if they do not push the leftist narrative that all races are exactly the same mentally and spiritually (but, oddly, not physically), remain astoundingly silent in the face of it; this is because such falsification only benefits the Jews (and, thus, their flunkies).

39 For what constitutes a healthy mind, body, and spirit, see *Myth and Sun: Essays of the ARCHETYPE*.

40 Nietzsche, *The Will to Power*, §246.

41 Serrano, *Adolf Hitler*, 770; emphasis added.

42 Serrano, *Adolf Hitler*, 82.

43 Serrano, *Hitler's UFO Against the New World Order* (article originally published August 1993), "The New World Order," 75.
44 Augustine of Hippo, *Enchiridion* (2002), 50.
45 "The most noble [slogan] known to us: *God helps those who help themselves!*" Adolf Hitler, 06 September 1938 (speech).
46 Joseph Goebbels, 05 June 1943 (speech). See T. Dalton's *Goebbels and the Jews* (2019) for extended passages.
47 *Fear and Trembling* (1983), 66.
48 Nietzsche, *Thus Spoke Zarathustra*, Part II, "Great Events."
49 Nietzsche, *The Will to Power*, §55.
50 Adolf Hitler, *Mein Kampf* vol. 2 (2019), "Worldview and Organization," 169; modified translation.
51 Serrano, *Adolf Hitler*, 844; emphasis added.
52 Adolf Hitler, *Mein Kampf* (Wewelsburg Archives, 2018), "Early Development of the NSDAP."
53 Spengler, *Man and Technics*, 10.
54 See *Hitler Avatāra* (2023) for more on the "leap of faith."
55 Spengler, *Man and Technics*, 86.
56 Serrano, *Adolf Hitler*, 83.
57 Spengler, *Man and Technics*, 84.
58 The statements are from Ed Bernays (Jew) and Ted Kaczynski (dissenter). Bernays' full quote: "The conscious and intelligent manipulation of the organized habits and opinions of the masses is an important element in democratic society. Those who manipulate this unseen mechanism of society constitute an invisible government which is the true ruling power of our country" (*Propaganda*, 37). For Kaczynski's full statement, see fn13 in this chapter.
59 The Jews' inimical nature will not even permit them to see the manipulative character of their countless talking heads, editors, authors, and advertisements pushing for the "#StandUpToJewishHate," "I Stand with Israel," "Blue Square," "Never Forget," or other anti-"antisemitism" movements.
60 *An ihrer inneren Zusammengehörigkeit änderte sich gar nichts.* Adolf Hitler, *Mein Kampf*, "Years of Study and Suffering in Vienna."
61 Spengler, *Man and Technics*, 85.
62 Spengler, *Man and Technics*, 87.
63 Serrano, *Manu*, 184.
64 Serrano, *Adolf Hitler*, 129.
65 Spengler, *Man and Technics*, 103.
66 Spengler, *Man and Technics*, 103.
67 "What is accelerationism, the theory believed in by U.S. white nationalists conspiring to attack its power grid?" (15 March 2023).

68 The misunderstanding is pervasive. See "Feral fascists and deep green guerrillas: infrastructural attack and accelerationist terror," *Critical Studies on Terrorism* (Loadenthal, 2022); "Riots, white supremacy, and accelerationism" (Byman, 2020); "White Supremacists Embrace Accelerationism" (ADL, 2019); etc. Materialists can never see beyond material.
69 Ovid, *Metamorphoses* (published as *Tales From Ovid*, 1998), translated by Ted Hughes, pp. 12, 10, 11, respectively.
70 See *Myth and Sun*.
71 See *Myth and Sun*.
72 Augustine of Hippo, *Enchiridion* (2002), 37.
73 Serrano, *Adolf Hitler*, 310.
74 Adolf Hitler, *Mein Kampf* vol. 1, "Nation and Race," 553.
75 Spengler, *Man and Technics*, 42.
76 "a rebel," *eines Empörers*. Spengler, *Man and Technics*, 42.
77 "have race," *Rasse haben*. Spengler, *Man and Technics*, 104; emphasis added.

— 3 —
The Figurative World

There is more to heaven and earth ... than can be imagined in your philosophy.
— William Shakespeare
Hamlet

1.

The length of each of the four *yugas* — or ages of the world — varies according to its tribulation; the closer a *yuga* is to God, the longer it lasts. This is a gift from God. The current Kali-Yuga, which is, among the *yugas*, most distant from the Divine, is purported to last 432,000 years. Preceding the Kali-Yuga is Dvāpara-Yuga; twice as long as its predecessor, its length is 864,000 years. Before this was Tretā-Yuga, which persists 1,296,000 years. And first was the Satya-Yuga, lasting 1,728,000 years. Thus, each age is separated from the next by 432,000 years. When the final, Kali *yuga*, whose end is ushered in by Kalki-Shiva, concludes, time will begin again with a new, Satya *yuga*. A thousand iterations of these *yugas* constitute a *kalpa*, or a day in the existence of Brahmā. Some have taken these spans literally, some figuratively. Time, however, being a phantom of the mind, must be understood figuratively.

The mind understands time linearly, but this too is a phantom — i.e., this is not a characteristic of time so much as it is an imposition of our mind, which we interpret as causality. Time, as the pure form of sensibility, gives context to our experience. It is through the inner sense of time that objects are subsumed under the rules of existence. Time is the *a priori* form of intuition serving as the link between appearances and our judgment.[1] This is all to say, again, that time is a phantom. Time is not linear any more than a raindrop or the sun is large. What we perceive is real to us, but not to Nature, not to God; we are Nature, but Nature is not we. Thus, our interpretation of time can never be more than this: we are captives of ourselves. This captivity, if we are aware of it, is the beginning of our awakening, for it prompts the self-reflection necessary to see the self, and thus the world, anew. We can transcend this captivity through a communion with that *will-to-life* and *-power* consummated in the being of the folk.

Hitler Avatāra[2] exists and existed as divine incarnation because his captivity was always *collective*, not individual — which is to say, his captivity was transcendent and, therefore, nonexistent: Hitler Avatāra is Nature, and Nature is Hitler Avatāra. To be nonexistent is to be in figurative time. Figurative time is our mind reaching for that which can never be attained, like Tantalus reaching for fruit that hangs ever beyond extended fingers. What is the difference between a nanometer and a light-year when movement is impossible? Nothing. We reach *nonetheless*. "To be German means to carry out a matter for its own sake."[3]

432,000 years represents that which is beyond reach. It is time, and time exists uniformly, simultaneously. Time is not linear. Linearity is demiurgical and is the root of Judaism, Judeo-Christianity, dialectical materialism, progressivism, and even scientism: linearity is Jewish perception imposed on a world beyond Jewish comprehension. The *real*, *time* itself, the *unseen seen* — these cannot be more than "spooky action at a distance" for the Jew.[4] Though it is not for lack of intelligence that the Jew cannot comprehend the incomprehensible, but lack of *faith*. Judeo-materialism is only a reflection of Demiurge-Jehovah's foul attempt at creation: it is a misunderstanding of transcendental beauty that will never measure up to the *real*.

But if time is not linear, we cannot therefore say that time is cyclical, for cyclicality is itself figurative. Time is beyond cyclicality; time is both from the mind (as intuition) and apart from the mind (as the noumenal condition foundational to intuition). To say time is cyclical, however, is to bring us within a nanometer of the tantalizing fruit, as opposed to the light-year distance at which we stand with linearity. What helps us bridge the gap and grasp the unreachable fruit is the final leap of faith. We break with materialism and move beyond time with faith. We commune with the infinite and exist in the figurative with faith. To exist in the figurative is to not exist at all.

432,000 can be distilled to 9 — the sacred, Aryan 9 that permeates Germanic mythos. Nine realms comprise the known-unknown world. Wotan sacrificed himself for nine nights, hanging on Yggdrasil for the revelation of the runes and nine mighty songs. The ninth sign learned by Wotan *sleeps the sea*. Heimdall, watchman of the gods, has nine mothers. Thor eats an ox and eight salmon in his attempt to retrieve Mjölnir. And on goes the myth, haven for the gods. Another number, 18, can be distilled to 9. The Mahabharata contains 18 *parvas*. The Bhagavad Gita has 18 chapters. The Pandavas lost their belongings to the Kauravas in 18 dice games. The Kurukshetra war is fought for 18 days with 18 armies. Each of the four commanders of the Kaurava army fought for 10, 5, 2, and 1 day(s), successively — each span halving the one before it — to match the 18 days. The Mahabharata is an epic invigorating the philosophy of the Vedas.

Veda, of Indo-European root, means *knowledge*, which was revealed to the conquering Aryans as they brought their northern ways south of the Black Sea. The Rig-Veda is the oldest of Hindu (Indo)-Aryan scriptures; *Rig* means *sacred*; Rig-Veda, then, is *sacred knowledge*. The "Rigsthula" — Song of Rig — of the *Edda* tells the story of Heimdall-Wotan[5] taking the name of "Rig" and visiting the daughters of men. From these visits came the three castes: slaves, peasants, and warriors; from the warriors came the kings. *Veda*, *Edda* — the former predates the latter — in form, but not in spirit. *Edda* stems from the Germanic *óthr*, meaning *poetry*. Knowledge (*Veda*) and poetry (*Edda*) are combined in a sacred mythos, one that transcends the form of materiality and manmade time. To be transcendent is to exist figuratively; and to exist figuratively is to not exist at all, which is to say, to exist in faith.

As the Paradox, He is an extremely unhistorical person. But this is the difference between poetry and reality: contemporaneousness.[6] We know the Paradox to be the Avatāra, who is only accessible through *faith*, which is to say, *contemporaneousness*.[7] When we see the number 9 recur, we are given the opportunity to see beyond Judeo-time, beyond linearity. We see instead the Aryan wheels of time intersecting and splicing in all four dimensions, pouring out from the four mouths of Brahmā. From these four mouths of four dimensions, we are given the revelation of the *sleeping sea — eternity*. The Prasna Upanishad reveals:

> Those who in search of the inner Spirit follow the spiritual path of the North with steadiness, purity, faith, and wisdom attain the regions of the sun. And there is the ocean of life, the refuge supreme, the land of immortality where there is no fear.[8]

The North is the abode of the sun, whose sign is the holy Swastika. The wisdom that lies beyond the north wind, blowing south across the blackened, churning sea exists *now*. It is the eternal sea of history that bears out even in quantum wave function: all exists simultaneously. It is the Black Sun that rises over the Black Sea.

Wotan *sleeps the sea* with his ninth song and sign,[9] which flows from the spirit of the *fourth* — that 2 which is half of 5. Karna, who is honor and loyalty incarnate, was one of the four Kaurava commanders and led his army for the *two-days-which-is-half-of-five*. Where is the missing time? It exists beyond our intuition, beyond materiality. For Karna's "duty was not to die, but to be faithful and loyal to the end, [thus becoming] the inspiration for all those *faithful* and *loyal*, and in this way, would embody what it means to *love*."[10]

Materiality and linearity — abodes of the Judeo-system — are the dead ends of life and love. What we see beyond even our intuition — we who defend the figurative edge of the last nanometer before it slips into the figures of materiality — is the *unseen*; what we know is the *unknown*; what we live is the *unlived*; what we fight is the *unfought*; what we love is the *unloved*.

The walls of Valhalla are graced with 540 doors — this, too, distills to 9. From each of these 540 doors go 800 fighters, the *Einherjar*. Day after day the *Einherjar* fulfill their duty — to live, fight, and die for the Idea. What is the Idea? It is *Honor* and *Loyalty* — the *faith* that compels them to leave the sanctuary of the Great Hall and fight to the death the faith-devouring Fenrir.

> Five hundred doors | and forty there are,
> I ween, in Valhall's walls;

> Eight hundred fighters | through one door fare
> When to war with the wolf they go.[11]

The *Einherjar* fulfill their duty by fulfilling their duty; they live, fight, and die for the faith that compels them to do the same. This is not tautological; it is the mystery of mythos. The mystery deepens: 800 *Einherjar* from each of the 540 doors is 432,000 — the span of years separating each of the *yugas* and the length of Kali-Yuga.

Take care not to see the time, but only the figures — and, far more importantly, only the *sign* and *song* of the figures, for therein lies the *figurative*, the nonexistent *being*. Commune with the mystifying mythos, inhere within the age-igniting fire — this is the meaning of all beginning, the mystery of all meaning, and the beginning of all mystery.

What exists after word is deed, and in deed dwells the danger. The danger is within you, and it consumes man and machine.

2.

The Aryan and the figurative embrace like boon companions. Where they have lost touch, there is only degradation. For the Aryan, the figurative is link to the Divine; it is the Third Eye. The essence of Hitlerism — as was demonstrated in its highest form in the *Schutzstaffel* (SS), and in the sanctuaries of the *Ordensburgen* (Order Castles) — is a communion with the Divine through the memory of the blood. This was not and is not a crass obsession with material race; this was and is a deep understanding of the fundamentality of race as the beginning of everything. From this fundament the true Aryan arises.

When race is seen as the beginning of everything, only then can refinement of character within the capacity of the race occur. Hitler's Reich-leaders studied at the *Nationalpolitische Erziehungsanstalten*, the *Adolf Hitler Schulen*, and the *Ordensburgen* where they would reconnect with the same spirit that created the Vedas, the *Edda*, and the spiritual-aristocracy that birthed the *Führerprinzip*.[12] The schools at which they studied and, indeed, all buildings of Hitler's Reich were meant to display "*superhuman magnitude* and to inspire *knightly actions*"[13] both inside and out. The Third Reich was meant to be the Aryans' recovery of the Third Eye. It was to be "where the *Sonnenmenschen*, the men of the Black Sun, were able to recover the lost organ of *Vril*, the direct knowledge of the memory of the blood."[14] The Black Sun: *die Schwarze Sonne* — the SS. A former student of the Order Castles tells us the meaning of the memory of the blood:

> We have gathered from all regions of the German *Volk*, to spend a year together here. We are at an age at which the learning period is generally assumed over, in which most have started to work independently. A majority of us have already founded a household.... Now that we have left profession and family and gathered here, it shows the awareness that *there is a duty beyond our individual lives, the duty towards the people.*[15]

The memory of the blood is the beginning of everything; it is our connection with past and future; it is the awareness that all time is figurative and imposed upon our material senses by a mind that is only a *medium*, a *vessel*, a *pathway* to a higher reality. Spiritual-aristocracy is built upon overcoming — it is the philosophy of *nonetheless*. One can connect with all time through the medium of the mind because all time exists simultaneously; there is no past, present, or future beyond the confines of the material mind; there is only the Divine. Language, whose construct lies within the parameters of material existence, can only get one so near divine communion, like a groping around in the dark.

But we persist nonetheless; for language, pushed within the figurative to the brink of oblivion, inspires great action. The only action one needs is the break with understanding, the leap of faith. If one cannot make the leap, one will remain a slave to the Judeo-system and its concomitant linearity.

Judaism, or Judeo-ism, is godlessness; it is materiality. Jews will never understand the figurative because they, being byproducts of Jehovahistic hate, have no capacity for faith; and though they might speak allegorically, this allegory only ever has a material end. "It all started with Moses Mendelsohn, who claimed Judaism to be a perfect

Enlightenment-like religion because ... he conceived it as a rational moral teaching without any supernatural illusions."[16] Feuerbach later observed the spiritually bereft nature of the Jew: "[The Jews'] ... God is ... *egoism*."[17] Marx, too, detected the baseness of the Jew, something he was intimately familiar with: "What is the secular basis of Judaism? *Practical need, selfishness*. What is the secular cult of the Jew? *Haggling*. What is his secular god? *Money*."[18] Marx continues:

> The Jew has emancipated himself in a Jewish manner, not only because he has acquired financial power, but also because, through him ... money has become a world power and the practical Jewish spirit has become the practical spirit of the Christian nations. The Jews have emancipated themselves insofar as the Christians have become Jews.[19]

Marx considers this a wholly *Jewish* way of achieving emancipation: the Jew does not raise itself over the "Christians" (i.e., the Europeans) because it *cannot*; instead, the Jew tears down and uproots the Europeans, thereby undercutting whatever remains of their spiritual-cultural identity to serve its own materialistic needs. It is the essence of the parasite; it is population as technics. Its innate *huckster-ness* is not only the Jew's crime against the host society, but it also marks a spiritual-cultural deviance. Because the European communities upon which it preys rest on a spiritual-cultural foundation, Jewish materiality erodes the spiritual (or figurative) essence of the European host. In this way, the Jew is guilty of spiritual-cultural (i.e., racial) deviance and religious impiety, along with socioeconomic crime.

To in part understand Jewish materiality, one must understand *usury*, which is the quintessence of Jewish character. Lending money on interest is synonymous with Jewry going back to antiquity. Usury itself is a lie: it presents to the swindled client a false picture of the funds to be reclaimed. *Take this money*, says Shylock, *and grow your business; I want only your flesh in return*. The client thinks he enters the relationship in good faith; his gullibility is the Jew's liquor, however; for behind the window-price lurks the *inter-*

est. A Jew's *interest* is material gain for self, spiritual loss for the other, and dominion over all. It is not a dominion for creative glory, as is the wont of Aryans; but only a parasitical dominion — one of gain until void, sup until death. When the host dies, the parasite relocates and lives to feed again.

Where the Aryan uses the figurative as the means to commune with God, the Jew uses it as naught but a clever soothing of its demiurgical ego — the Jew sees *I* and *Thou*, but never God. Martin Buber, patron saint of Judeo-philosophy, regards the Germanic philosophy of Meister Eckhart as an *annihilation of self*. Indeed it is, in the sense that the self is only fulfilled when it communes with the transcendent — but this is something the Jew can never fathom. For the Jew there is only *I* (the *Chosen*) and *Thou* (the *goyim*), and the relationship between them underlies all. There is of course the "it" in Buber's Judeo-worldview, but it stands as only the implement whereby the *I-Thou* relationship is manipulated. From an existential standpoint, it is the Jew's aim to eliminate the "it" altogether, thus exalting and intensifying the *I-Thou* dynamic; the Jew thereby aspires to make an implement of "thou" — population as *tool*, as *technics*, which further materializes the relationship.

Not only do the *I* and *Thou* engage in a material, *quid-pro-quo* way, the *I* and *Thou* also supplant the metaphysical, the spiritual. In his book *Kingship of God* (1932), Buber pretends to acknowledge the sovereignty of "God," citing Judges 8:22-23, by saying divine authority cannot be transferred to man; this stands in contrast to Carl Schmitt's political theology and the Germanic tradition undergirding the *Führerprinzip*, wherein divine authority, hard-won, is delegated to or embodied in the sovereign. Buber would like to think that no man could take the divine mantle — that the Jew somehow abstains from power by rebuffing any divine authority manifested in the individual. What this means, however, is that the individual is denied as an agent of the Divine and that the Divine is instead realized through the body politic, which itself is comprised of the *I*, which is to say, "the Chosen," the Jew.

This is a rejection of the Third Reich as Third Eye — which is to say, a rejection of the Aryan figurative world — and it is an acceptance of the Judeo-system, wherein the Zionist cause and its material support from Gentile nations sits at the heart of a globalist movement.

In Judges 8, which Buber cites, Gideon declines the Israelites' wish that he become king — but he does have "one request":

> "that each of you give me an earring from your share of the plunder." ... They answered, "We'll be glad to give them." So they spread out a garment, and each of them threw a ring from his plunder onto it. The weight of the gold rings he asked for came to seventeen hundred shekels [i.e., 43 lbs., or 20 kg], not counting the ornaments, the pendants and the purple garments worn by the kings of Midian or the chains that were on their camels' necks. Gideon made the gold into an ephod [i.e., a garment worn by Jewish priests], which he placed in ... his town. All Israel prostituted themselves by worshiping it there...[20]

Thus it happened that the Jew forwent leadership for shekels; thus it happened that the Jews worshipped the shekels. Moreover, Buber cannot discuss this event "scientifically at all."[21] Instead, he is content to stop with the event's *possibility*, which is his acceptance of its allegorical nature. The Aryan divines the Jewish allegory's meaning: real power rests in money and this must be apotheosized.

Contrast this with the Hindu-Aryan Bhagavad Gita: "A man of understanding acts with mind and intelligence perfectly controlled, [giving] up all sense of proprietorship over his possessions and acts only for the bare necessities of life..."[22] Or here:

> Four kinds of pious men render devotional service unto Me: the distressed, the desirer of wealth, the inquisitive, and he who is searching for knowledge of the Absolute. Of these, the wise one who is in full knowledge in union with Me through pure devotional service is the best. For I am very dear to him, and he is dear to Me.[23]

Similar examples abound. And here is the Aryan *Edda*: "no joy | the gold shall give thee, (The rings shall soon | thy slayers be)..."[24] Or here:

> Sigmund and all his sons were far above all other men in might and stature and courage and every kind of ability. Sigurth, however, was the foremost of all, and all men call him in the old tales the noblest of mankind and the mightiest leader.[25]

Material does not make a man great or a noble leader; his character and ability do. And a man's innate, hereditary character is refined by his attunement to the transcendent. When one proves himself worthy of the transcendent, as a representative of his folk, he demonstrates the capacity to assume leadership, which is to say, to manifest as God's authority — God's representative of the transcendent will of a folk — amongst his people. This is the Third Eye that sees beyond the *Veil of Maya*. The prioritization of character and the view that one's race and bearing were windows to the soul were concepts that routinely saw articulation and concretization in Hitler's Reich. One such articulation was the foundation of Hitlerist leadership schools:

> A high degree of racial value and faultless characteristics, matched with determination, willpower and readiness for action are requirements that must be met by each political leader. Furthermore, a disposition for above-average performance and good appearance which compliments and rounds off the personality is absolutely essential, so that the political leader, through the combination of his inner and outer attitude, can lead the *Volk* and have its absolute acceptance.[26]

Those who meet the requirements stipulated above are the *exception*, not the rule. Even in Hitler's time, such a man (or woman on the home front) was a rarity — so it stands to reason that such a man (or woman) is even more rare today. Yet so many seem to imagine that simply displaying the Swastika is sufficient for contemporary "qualification" — it is definitely *not*. "White" skin qualifies you for *nothing* — especially today when so many "whites" are nothing more than loudmouthed dreck. *Garbage is garbage*, regardless of skin color. But all of this is just more sign of the time: If many competent, quality "whites" existed, we would not be living in the Kali-Yuga.

What this means is that Jewish distortions must be exorcised from oneself and the larger Aryan community. For oneself, this is done by being fit — mentally, physically, and spiritually.[27] This takes discipline, decency, honor, and loyalty. For the community, this is done by ending the Judeo-system. The Aryan and Jew can coexist if necessary, but they can never have equilibrium: one must dominate the other, for the two are antithetical to each other; when one lives according to its inner drive, the other suffers.

Ideally, Aryan and Jew will neither cohabitate nor coexist. If the Aryan eradicates the Jew, both the Aryan and the Jew will benefit: the Aryan will fulfill its spiritual-cultural destiny without distortion and the Jew will be put out of its existential misery — i.e., its servitude to Satan-Jehovah will be ended, at least in this realm. If the Jew eradicates the Aryan, only the Aryan will benefit: the Aryan spirit will be freed from the burden of Jewish spiritual-cultural distortions, but the Jewish parasite will lose its preeminent host — it will turn on itself and self-destruct.

The fear of this scenario terrorizes the Jew: this is why it is so *obsessively overbearing* with its cries of "anti-Semitism," its fantastical Holocaust bludgeon, its relentless anti-Germanic propaganda and obligatory accompanying memorials, its "Jewish centers" on campuses and in neighborhoods across the West, etc. The Jew wants to dominate and wants everyone to agree with this domination — i.e., because of its parasitical nature, it prefers not to eradicate actual or potential hosts; it will only move to eradication of the host (Aryan) if the host (Aryan) begins to awaken to the quite obvious Jewish supremacy over the modern world. The Aryan will never awaken to this, however, unless it is fit, in the fullest sense of the word, and lives with an eye on the figurative — i.e., has faith.

What is important here is that *the Aryan has nothing to lose in either situation*; thus, it only works to the overall Aryan benefit if we fight the Jew and its diabolical system at every turn — for we will either reverse the present situation and dominate the Jew, or we will heroically die trying and knowingly exterminate the Jew anyway. Destiny tells us the former course is closed to us — for there is no "us."

You must therefore fight to the end, bold Aryan — *nonetheless!*

3.

Karl Löwith met his former teacher Martin Heidegger at a café for coffee. It was early-1930s Germany; Löwith was Jewish, Heidegger a staunch Hitlerist. They talked personal affairs, philosophy, and the current *Zeitgeist*. Löwith mentioned his concern over the changing times; Heidegger understood and offered his intellectual support. Glinting in a sunray that escaped from behind the clouds was Heidegger's Swastika lapel pin.

How could Heidegger have taught, conversed with, and carried on a friendship with Löwith, a Jew, and maintained his belief in the Hitlerian Idea? Simple: Heidegger was a thinking being and not a senseless thug.

Are you offended at the Jew, Aryan? You must be blinded by the "whiteness" of your skin. Learning opportunities abound. If you refuse them, you refuse improvement, which is to say, you refuse God. The Hitlerist moves, like Mao among the people, as a fish through water. One would never know he or she exists. Heidegger could wear the lapel pin because complete political victory was seemingly in reach. Destiny had other plans. With the world stacked against him, the present Hitlerist must live without sign; this is possible because the Idea is branded on the Hitlerist soul. Pins have been discarded for something more meaningful. As Heidegger said later in life, *only a god can save us*.[28] Serrano put it this way:

> I have Jewish friends, and even though we do not see things the same way I keep correspondence with more than a few of them. They have not stopped greeting me despite my views and combats. Perhaps they also admire me as an open enemy who has discovered their

plans and the lies their truth reveals. They do admire those they want to destroy. Hence their fascination for Hitler. They cannot stop being drawn toward him, hypnotized by him, realizing that all, in the end, favors the resurrection of his Myth.[29]

Senseless thugs outnumber even learning opportunities in this Kali-Yuga. What is a senseless thug? *An adrift child in an adult's body.* The world is full of adult children just waiting for the Jew to tell them what to think and how to act. When one of these adult children, these Judeo-bots, becomes attracted to the exoteric trappings of the Hitlerian Idea, this only ever works in the favor of the Judeo-system — for now we have a jack-booting thug incapable of perpetuating the myth, incapable of even comprehending the myth, and the Jew smiles. This is why the headlines are ever filled with "anti-Semitic" tropes: the Jew dreams of the senseless thug providing fuel for the fire animating the Judeo-bots.

Of course, even when senseless thugs do not exist, the Jew creates them. This is why, for example, the *Wall Street Journal* can run an article entitled "The Global War on Jews"[30] without irony. Jewry must feed the beast.

The beast is the population and technics; it is the exploitative instinct of the Jew galvanizing the will of the people into a Jehovahistic hammer to destroy the world. The point of "The Global War on Jews" article, like every article concocted by the Jew, is clear: pro-Jewish action = *safety, democracy, innocence,* and *survival*; anti-Jewish action – *barbarism, violence, catastrophe, Holocaust, danger, hate, genocide.* Every Jew-backed story published today — which is to say, *any* story in this Judeo-world — has the same goal: manipulate mass emotion to favor Jewish domination. This is done through fear. Satan-Jehovah feeds off the fear and blood its golems rouse to a manic boil.

4.

Platonic Idealism, or Plato's theory of the Forms, postulates an *unseen actual* — a world beyond our sensory experience that nonetheless forms the basis of our experience. The *form* of a horse, for instance, outlines the nature of the horse, and all specific instances of any individual horse are derived from this template. The same can be said of any animate or inanimate object available to perception.

Immanuel Kant took the *unseen actual* and incorporated transcendentalism — i.e., an examination of the ways of understanding both the perceived and perception itself. Similar to the Platonic Forms was the Kantian noumenal world, or that world which is ever beyond our literal reach, but which stands as the fundament for all phenomena. Kant reasoned that space and time themselves are products of the mind and, thus, so is causality. Time, much like space, is a *product* of a mode of existence; it does not exist as perceived apart from the perceiver.

Arthur Schopenhauer, while rejecting Kant's noumenal-phenomenal distinction, continued the Idealism tradition and nevertheless posited an *unseen* (but not unfelt) *actual* world. Schopenhauer's world mirrored Hobbes' "nasty, brutish, and short" existence, but behind the struggle was an unrelenting, blind (irrational) will: the *will-to-live*. The neat Forms of Plato and noumenal niceties of Kant, with Schopenhauer, became the raw, wild will.

> Space and time are the many-colored glass that stains the white radiance of eternity. Once this glass is broken, once the veil of Maya (illusion) is rent, there is seen to be no difference between a thing that exists here and now and another thing that exists at some remote place in space and time. All reality is a single striving.[31]

A single striving — man might as well just be along for the ride and, if he is smart, will just slip into nonexistence without polluting the world with more consciousness blind to the blind will.

Friedrich Nietzsche, appalled at Schopenhauer's quite un-Germanic (i.e., Buddhistic) approach to managing the will, embraced the unadulterated energy of the will and turned it into a *will-to-power* — something that simply cannot *be* without man's agency. There exists the seen world for Nietzsche, and the unseen world is only the internal compulsion manifested as external devotion: *This world is a will to power — and nothing besides!*³² It is *the world as will*, for both Schopenhauer and Nietzsche.

Later, Carl Jung saw the will as a collective fulfillment of a spiritual-cultural form — the Archetype. "Archetype is an explanatory paraphrase of the Platonic εἶδος."³³ Each generation has a reckoning with what it considers "the gods." Unable to recognize the self- and system-imposed order of time, man sees the gods fade as time progresses; or rather, he sees, as Ovid noted, "a new god." "In reality, however, he has merely discovered that up till then he has never thought about his [gods] at all. And when he starts thinking about them, he does so with the help of what he calls *reason*..."³⁴

Disappearance of the gods results from an inability or unwillingness to perceive time as figurative, to instead commit to a faithless existence in the illusion of the "real." It is servitude to the Judeo-system, for this system fosters both the inability and unwillingness to confront oneself, to pursue as an end in itself *self-awareness, mindfulness* — that dredging up of the figurative space from deep within one's being, that sharing of (un)consciousness both *imbued with* and *distinct from* time. It is the gods within who are denied when one is caught up in the "real," the veil of perception. But this is only to say that one's self is denied, which is precisely what the Jew and its Satan-Jehovah desire. When one mocks the gods in favor of political solutions, only the vacant husk in the mirror is mocked.³⁵ "The mirror does not flatter, it faithfully shows whatever looks into it; namely the face we never show to the world because we cover it with the persona, the mask of the actor. But the mirror lies behind the mask and shows the true face."³⁶

What does the *mirror behind the mask* show? A faithless materialist trapped in a system controlled by the Jew. Jung, like his *contemporary* Spengler, never saw the Innocent Jew, however.³⁷ Jung's insight was his view into the timeless (un)consciousness that hitches us to the human, which, in its highest manifestation, is a tether to the gods.

> Thoughtfulness, or mindfulness, imbues our life and action with the meaning necessary to *fight* and thus *realize* what it means to be fully human: that humanity

without God is mere biological machinery destined for drab mediocrity.[38]

This was perhaps Jung's lesson.

What each of these five philosophers grasps in their unique way is the Hindu-Aryan *Veil of Maya*, or veil of perception/illusion. There is a "real" world of perception, and an underlying *unseen actual* world of *reality*. Perhaps not surprisingly, the real world for these thinkers was the unseen, almost figurative world. This *unseen actual* represents, for the Aryan, a connection with the Divine: there is something more than what this world of perception has to offer. This does not mean we plunge into an existence of lethargy and apathy; rather, it means we live thoughtful lives, contemplating the *unseen actual*, in order to commune with supra-sensory reality. The pathway to this supra-sensory reality is, naturally, not our senses, but that sense which is not a sense, that eye which is not an eye — the Third Eye.

It is with clarity that we discern with the Third Eye — which is to say, that we commune with God. Clarity only comes with focus on the transcendent that remains unblemished by individuation. That is, it is purity of heart, and purity of heart is to will one thing.

> Reason is the means for a man of faith to further the will of God. God's will is the Good. The Good is that which transcends and uplifts; it is sacrificing oneself for the benefit of the whole that reflects oneself; this reflection is physical, mental, and spiritual; the Good is *one thing*. Purity of heart is to will one thing. The Good is singular; it is *willing one thing*....
>
> An individual united in faith *with* and *in* his folk wills one thing: the continued existence and thriving of his blood as it is reflected in his kinsmen.[39]

Clarity is communion and communion is clarity: this is the *one thing* that stands behind the veil — the *illusion* — of perception. The tautology of the real is the *unseen actual*; it is the figurative world that coaxes our inward drive to combat in this Cosmic Struggle.

5.

Agamemnon battled Troy with Demios (dread) and Phobos (fear) on his shield.[40] His goal was to instill fear: the great Aryan warrior-king — "blond, large, and powerful ... eloquent, wise, and noble"[41] — used his weapons of war to demoralize and defeat his enemy before the fight had even begun, *for in all battles it is the eye which is first vanquished.*[42] Demios was called upon to terrorize the rival before the battle; Phobos was invoked to spread panic among the opponent during the battle.

Agamemnon's implements, as an Aryan in an Aryan battle, were sword and shield — inanimate weapons of men against the contrivances of other men, strength against strength. *The weapons and the battle share their essence with the character of the combatant, and one is not divisible from the other. Life and the tools one uses to navigate it flow from the inward drive of those destined to confront it. The inward drive of the Aryan is creation; the inward drive of the Jew is destruction. Each combatant fulfills its role in the Cosmic Struggle.*[43]

Agamemnon used Demios and Phobos figuratively, as symbols on his shield and untamed aggression in his eyes to fight his opponent *man to man*. In this way, Agamemnon engages in real combat to commune with the gods, the Divine; likewise, he fulfills his duty and communes with the gods by engaging his opponent in combat — such is Aryan symmetry. Life is struggle and struggle is life; it is through struggle that we realize our potential and reach the *unseen actual*, that we fulfill our duty by apprehending meaning through faith; it is through this faith that we reach the Divine, and it is through the Divine that we muster the faith to continue the struggle — *for all time*. Arjuna did not witness the splendor of God until he accepted his duty and waged battle against his foes. Aryans are men and women of strength, and they use implements of their creation to battle their enemies.

6.

Demios and Phobos can be used in other ways, however. Fearmongering is ubiquitous in the Americanized West: wherever exists the Jew, there also exists fear.[44] All arms of the Judeo-system — media, medicine, academia, finance, and government — flex and spring to blanket the masses with the dread of *what was, what is,* and *what will be.* Fear is implemented to turn the mass itself into an implement: weaponization of the herd — the mechanization of men — is the primary aim. In states of psychological frenzy, stupor, or impotence the masses can be effectively manipulated for the desired aim. It is the methodology of any abuser.

There are two basic kinds of fear spread among the herd: (1) fear for the Jew, and (2) fear for livelihood. The latter has broader appeal so is more widely used: everyone is innately concerned for what affects them directly, so the Judeo-system exploits this natural concern by both portraying it as constantly under threat and actually creating the conditions for its being threatened. Newscast "alerts," pandemics and endemics, equity initiatives, economic downturns, territorial disputes and border crises — these are but a few of the springing arms of systemic fear.

Fear for the Jew, on the other hand, is more precise, more acute: the Jew is always elevated as distinct among the races for its "tortured" history. *Fear for the Jew* is the suffering of all Aryan-oppressed people condensed into the being of the most important race in the linear history of the Judeo-system, and the arms of this system take great care in curating the cause of the Jew: *what was —* Holocaust; *what is* — anti-Semitism; *what will be* — Holocaust: these are the fabricated fears for the Jew, and the agents of the Judeo-system ensure everyone is aware of them all the time.

While these are the practical uses of Demios and Phobos in the Judeo-system, the Jew has a secret. Fear is for *manipulation*, the turning of man into implement, yes — but it is also food for the Demiurge, for Satan-Jehovah. Every newscast "alert," every maudlin fiction vomited by Judeo-Hollywood, every feigned or manufactured crisis, is naught but bait to elicit a specific emotional response: fear.[45] These are not isolated events or happenstance; these are Judeo-rituals in tribute to the Lord of Darkness. Fear is the foreplay to ritualistic bloodshed. Time and again do the fear-drums bang out the rhythm of marching armies, criminal mobs, and "peaceful" protestors: It is the organized chaos that riles and lulls the hive-mind as needed. Serrano warned us:

> Death is the oven that cooks the Demiurge's food. Material dissolves into yet more material, energy revolves around, transforms, and from pain there rises thick vapors that strengthen him. His greatest joy is extracted from suffering.[46]

The smoldering rubble within the Judeo-system strengthens the very anchor of the Judeo-system. The Lord of Darkness is lord of spiritual destruction; when the spirit is destroyed, only a husk remains; from the husks an anthill is erected, a hive-mind is conjured, and a demon dominates. Thus spoke Jehovah to his Jews:

> This very day I will begin to put the terror and fear of you on all the nations under heaven. They will hear reports of you and will tremble and be in anguish because of you....[47]
>
> And when the Lord your God has delivered them over to you and you have defeated them, then you must destroy them totally. Make no treaty with them, and show them no mercy.... [Instead,] break down their altars, smash their sacred stones, ... and burn their idols in the fire. For you are a people holy to the Lord your God. The Lord your God has chosen you out of all the peoples on the face of the earth to be his people, his treasured possession.[48]

From the beginning, the Jews and Satan Jehovah have made it their aim to sow fear among the Gentiles. There are no more diabolical people on this planet than the Organic Lies, the Breathing Hate — the Innocent Jews. Fear is the source of their strength and its consequent spiritual death will not end until the Judeo-system falls.

From Chaos comes Kronos, from void comes time. Kronos crafts the Jew, the Jew fulfills Kronos, and following the Jew is *pandemonium*, chaos reanimated in demonic scene. With dread, discord, and distraction the Jew rips the mind away from the figurative and shoves it into the "real," the chaos of our current underworld, into the linearity that grips the neck like a leash, like a noose. With noosed necks the masses march down the path of time, down into the dregs of the universe to be collected at the bottom of time by the Judaized Electric Messiah who directs "the electronic energy that is the food of Satan."[49]

Shouldering their Demiurge-Messiah, the Jews mimic the figurative with ever-updated technological devices — the herd roams urban pastures with illuminated faces held captive by the electric bars of glowing pixels. Energy and information disseminated from these portable prisons illuminates the illuminated, and everyone is "enlightened." *Mass Phobos-hypnosis* infects and directs the unthinking actions of the *illuminated* herd: "the subliminal messages of television, ... propaganda and drugs that facilitate the use of suggestion in the psyches of the multitudes ... are introduced in drinks, [foods,] and pharmacopoeia that Macro-Capitalism controls worldwide." The energies of this soul-destroying medley "pass through our bodies *as if we did not exist*, as if they were imagining us."[50] *As if they were imagining us.*

We are *imagined* if we give up the struggle and abandon the figurative. One who eschews the nonexistent being of the figurative slips into the rigid figures of the "real," the "actual," wherein all unthinking action uplifts, not the soul, but the satanic senses imposing imaginary time. The Judeo-system creates machines, not men. And when one succumbs to the trappings of the "real," one *ceases to be*, in the meaningful sense.

The "real" is the tomb of the dreck, the currency of the Judeo-system, the dark energy turning living beings into translucent husks of fading light. Engorged on this *fading*, the Lord of Darkness crafts new generations of imaginary imitations of servants who do with pleasure the will of their master.

7.

When through the Universe the order was given to act in unison against Hitler, [the herd of White Traitors] could not do otherwise than obey, by hypnosis, compulsion of their blood, fear and even stupidity.

But that should not lead us to lose sight of the principal culprits: the International Jew, mythic and planetary — and his Demiurge, Jehovah. Great efforts are being made at present, as in the past, to cover it up, trying to draw attention away from this subversion, [that is the work of] the same "White Traitors." But let us not deceive ourselves, because all of them are no more than submissive and obedient collaborators of the Jew here on earth and their Demiurge beyond the earth. They are under his strict command, working for him and to extend his planetary domination. They are also his victim and food at the end of the *Manvantara*. Because the mythical, unswerving Jew despises them as traitors, and their Demiurge will eat them too.

If the Demiurge discovered in time that he was going to lose the war, he would order his Jew golem to destroy the earth before allowing its transmutation. And he would do the same with his illusory Universe. But that is already of no importance, since he lost that opportunity. *The Avatar of the Führer has already won the war*. Only the Demiurge and the Jew do not know it.[51]

So held Serrano. How *could* the Demiurge and the Jew know? They are *products*, *imitations* of creation — material imitations of the nonexistent being of the figurative, the *unseen actual*.

The Jew and its Judeo-bots cling to the falsity of imitation because it *is* real to them; they neither know, nor can know anything besides the veil of perception. The Jew loves — no, *worships* — the *material* because there is nothing beyond the material for it: physical death is the end of the product without a soul. So the Jew apotheosizes the manufactured drama of daily life — through the media, through academia, through government; it is all nonsensical drama so the Jew can feel *something* before it meets an end in the thresher-jaws of Satan-Jehovah. Unable to extract itself from the "politico-social delusional systems," the Jew instead fans these subsystems under the umbrella of its overarching worldview into a seething turbulence, wherein the *gods*, the *Third Eye*, the *soul* are replaced with an "unparalleled impoverishment of symbolism," "a new problem."[52]

The Jew solves this problem by imposing its hell upon the herd, attacking every instance of Aryan beauty, determined to eradicate the memory of its planetary servitude and diabolical origin. The Jew was born in demiurgical ugliness and remains ugly, outwardly and inwardly: 6-shaped noses, fleshy lips, and round faces; spiteful, envious, whiny and base. And Jews must maintain "their animal characteristics ... as signs of their election ... by their infrahuman Demiurge."[53] To mask this stain of their heritage, however, they ravage European blood — in bedrooms, boardrooms, and war rooms. *The Jew hates the beauty of Nature because this beauty is a nostalgia for Hyperborea.*[54]

Benton Bradberry recalls how the blood-ritual known as the Russian Revolution, for instance, saw the Judeo-Marxists

> especially interested in handsome boys and pretty girls. These were the first to be killed. It was believed that there would be more intellectuals among attractive people.... The Semites, jealous of white beauty, massacred beautiful whites...[55]

Now every Gentile is a pawn in the Jews' game: you are a means to an end, and that end is a prolonging of the ugly, soulless existence standing between the Jew and its terrifying return to the bowels of Satan-Jehovah.

Is it hard to believe this revaluation of all "reality"? Does *understanding* or "*reason* — which in point of fact is nothing more than the sum total of all ... prejudices and myopic views" preclude your acceptance of the reality that stands beyond "reality"?[56] Fear not, for you stand at the brink of faith: "It is only the things we don't understand that have any meaning."[57]

8.

A family of European descent detached from society and escaped to the wilderness. They held a deep, soul-stirring conviction their teenaged son was somehow instrumental in the Second Coming of Christ. A friend of the family did not share this belief and reported their disappearance to authorities; he then circulated various media outlets sharing his story. The outlets, interested in the sensational nature of the event and advertisement revenue, broadcast the friend's story. "What drove the family to make such a rash decision, and do you share their faith?" the family friend was asked during an interview. Before he could answer, a commercial interrupted the program: it was an advertisement targeting children and their parents — to buy an artificially sweetened, flavored, and colored *treat*.

What is real in this story? What can the illuminated do with nooses around their necks that tighten to the droning rhythm of a hive-mind?

Bava Metzia (114b) of the Talmud tells the story of a Jewish "Master," or rabbi, in a Gentile cemetery. *What is the reason that the Master is standing in a cemetery?* asks the teacher. The student responds "that the graves of gentiles do not render one impure, as it is stated: *And you, My sheep, the sheep of My pasture, are man* (Ezekiel 34:31), which teaches that you, i.e., the Jewish people, are called *man*, but gentiles are not called *man*." The question is never answered — *Why is the rabbi in the Gentile cemetery?* Perhaps a ritual to the Lord of Darkness is underway, or perhaps a searching for useable parts for some new golem. We will never know because we are only reminded of the Jews' special standing with Satan-Jehovah. Indeed: Gentiles — especially Aryans — have no standing with Satan-Jehovah, so why seek it like so many do? In the end they are only seen as traitors by even the Jews themselves, destined to serve as demiurgic food.

What is real in this story? What can the illuminated do with nooses around their necks that tighten to the droning rhythm of a hive-mind?

9.

The only remaining *real* is the *unreal*. The only remaining *solution* is the *dissolution*. All else is food for the Demiurge. End the Judeo-system and the noose is loosed.

What do you have to *gain* from this fight, Aryan? Hitler knew what you had to *lose*:

> You can give up everything else, since you will be laughed at and ridiculed and persecuted. You must be aware that you will be without bread, that they will throw you out of everywhere. You will have nothing of which you can be certain, other than death perhaps. But you see before you something for which we all fight.[58]

These "losses" are only the trappings of the "real," of the Judeo-system that means to ensnare and enslave the fighters and fodder in this Cosmic Struggle. Your gain, however, is the Jews' loss, which is to say, you have *everything* to gain. This is our only concern. Behind every attack against Aryans and Aryan lifeways "stands the hate-filled power of our Jewish foe, a foe to whom we had done no harm but who attempted to subjugate and make [the Germanic folk] its slave..."[59] Behind every attack against the Judeo-system stands the honor- and loyalty-loving Aryan, who attempts to free creation from its subjugation under the Jewish heel.

Attack the "real" and free the figurative. The world will never be the same, for it will burn in the fires of faith.

10.

The line between love and hate is nebulous and laden with meaning. There is an Indian aphorism that posits the question, "Who will more quickly reach perfection: He who loves God, or he who hates him?" The answer is *the man who hates God*; for the man who hates God thinks of him more often. Emotion is powerful and can lead to a great many things, even to many great things, if it is oriented on the transcendent.

The Cosmic Struggle — the war between Supreme Creator and Demiurge, Aryan and Jew, light and dark — is nebulous and laden with meaning. That the Jew is the Breathing Hate is clear: everything the Jew touches decays, and it deadens spirit everywhere in favor of a *materialistic idea* — the concretization of a noble faith.[60] The Jew institutionalizes and materializes any link to the Supreme Creator, and in this way trains its hate on *objects*, on things systematized within the delusional drama it constantly agitates to excite the fear it needs for sustenance. When the Jew uses allegory (e.g., the Torah) or the abstract (e.g., *liberty, equality, justice*), it is only as means to manipulate the objects of its hate. The Jew hates *things* — *material things* that stand in the way of its *material dominion* over the *material world*.

But the Jew cannot reach perfection, unless it is a perfection of sordidness; that is, unless it is a material perfection devoid of spirit and shine. The Jew's hate, therefore, is not elevating; it is degrading — for the *objects* of its hate. The Jew cannot reach perfection — i.e., the Divine — because the Jew itself is a *thing*, the crowning achievement of the Demiurge, and the Jew hates *things*, not God. Objects of existence trapped in the Judeo-system are degraded to a point of confinement whose walls are the cupped hands of the Jew.

The Jew's hatred of things, then, is only a hatred of self — a hatred of the cupped hands that are not one's own, but instead are the unclimbable, indestructible walls of a demiurgical Jericho. When the Jew looks outward, beyond the walls, it sees only desert sand melted into glassy mirrors: There in the distance is just the chasm of an empty self — a material existence that imitates the blank stare of a demon, a thief who carves a slice off creation and deems itself *God*.

No, perfection is not imitation; it is the wild leap across the chasm into the *unknown empyrean*, the *unseen actual*. Perfection is communion with God. In the aforesaid aphorism, the man who loves God attains perfection in seven lifetimes; the man who hates God reaches it in three. The ten lifetimes between them reduces to one: the *willing of one thing*: the *Good: perfection*.[61] Whether the Aryan loves or hates, his focus is on God. When the Aryan loves, he loves the strength of his folk; when the Aryan hates, he hates the weakness of his folk — *always* the focus is on his folk, on the epic in which he plays a part. In ten lifetimes the Aryans who love and hate will stand side by side against the demon's blank stare.

Ten lifetimes is *now*, Aryan. What do you see in the dark, demonic mien? It is the rising wall of a millennium, a bolt from the simultaneous blue, the molten roots of a tectonic shift — it is the hate of an Aryan unbound.

11.

Anna Plaim, housemaid of Hitler (1941-43), recounted some of the sacrifices those at the Berghof, quite distant from the Eastern Front, had to endure; these were sacrifices of comfort. For Adolf Hitler, as Führer and First Soldier, thought it inappropriate that the fighting men of Greater Germany should sacrifice so much while those comfortably behind the lines suffered little. One of the touchier matters for the ladies of the Berghof, Plaim recalled, centered on fur coats: "It was ... deemed inappropriate to wear fur coats while our soldiers froze to death in the Russian winter. That's why there was the call for everyone to donate their fur coats so that they could be sent to the front." This predicament "gave [the ladies] real headaches," for "these coats were much too valuable for the front."[62]

Hence it was impossible for the Reich to win the war: Those benefitting the most from the heroic sacrifices in the greatest *battle* of the greatest *struggle* in history couldn't be bothered to simply *commit* to the cause. It was *impossible* for the Reich to win the war, even at its zenith, because *losing was fated*: not everyone could make the necessary sacrifices because Destiny demanded they *pursue selfish ends here* and *betray their blood there*. From defeat came victory, for the heroic revelation vivified new souls born with open eyes.

Hesiod tells of the woeful Age of Iron, or what we might call the Judeo-system:

> Now truly is a race of iron. Men exhaust themselves with work and fret by day, and perish still by night; and the gods shall lay stinging woe upon them.... Zeus will destroy this race of mortal men when they come to have grey hair on their temples at birth. Fathers will not agree with their children, nor will the children agree with their fathers, ... comrade will stand against comrade, and brother against brother. Men will dishonor their parents and lose respect for the gods....
>
> Instead of good, men will praise the evildoer and his disturbed dealing. Quantity alone will be right, and reverence will cease to be; and the wicked will hurt the worthy man, speaking false words against him... Only

bitter sorrows will be left for mortal men, and there will be no help against evil.⁶³

No help against evil — because it is fated. The Aryan fight against this evil is also fated, however. So be bold, Aryan: *audentes Fortuna iuvat* — Fortune favors the bold; the gods enliven you. And if the destination as you embark on your fated mission is nothing other than the slopes of a newly erupted Vesuvius, this is *all the better*: for we should *live dangerously, and build our cities on the slopes of Vesuvius!*⁶⁴

Fate revealed the Jew and made martyrs out of the maligned. If martyrs inspire the ranks of both victor and vanquished in the Great Battle of this Cosmic Struggle, this is *all the better*; for it means we truly are on course for the final conflagration. Yes, heroes and martyrs, villains and vanities — all march to the same rhythmic compulsion.

Judeo-system:
Caterpillar and cocoon;
Shiva emerges.

Shiva emerges — this means honor and loyalty; this means you fulfill your duty, Aryan. "Carry out your prescribed duty of fighting. With your activities dedicated to Me and your mind and intelligence fixed on Me, you will attain Me without doubt." Thus spoke the Avatāra.⁶⁵

12.

An event of great import — *the greatest weight* — must now be conveyed. It is 1939; the fire is stoked, the cauldron is filled, and from the sky rolls the unspoken Word. Döhring recalls a dramatic day with Hitler:

> At the very moment of signing the pact in Moscow, all of us were standing on the terrace of the Berghof and came to behold an exceptional appearance in the sky, which spread over the Latten Mountains and the Untersberg. Everyone was transfixed by this horribly beautiful, but equally terrifying shape appearing in the

sky. First, the clouds shaded in various color tones ranging from sulfur-yellow to a fiery red to dark blue and then bulging into a deep black, then they literally came rolling toward the Obersalzberg. Those clouds did not move along normally, but would rotate and roll and tumble into one another — most unsettling....

I was never able to forget that particular day, since I was never again to experience something quite so scary. It took about a quarter of an hour for this horrible and gruesome sight to disappear....

There was a mysterious, elegant, blonde lady who was part of Hitler's private entourage. Her name was Marion Schönemann and she was a fortuneteller from Vienna. All of a sudden, she collapsed, and when she came to, she predicted, with all guests present: 'Mein Führer, this augurs nothing good. I saw blood, misery, distress, chaos and a cruel demise.' Hitler was totally shocked and responded to her: 'Yes, well, if it must happen, then let it happen as fast as possible. Goodbye, ladies and gentlemen.' He turned on his heels and disappeared into the Berghof.

It's up to everyone to interpret this even as they wish. Summer lightning, phenomena in the sky — caused by supernatural powers or perhaps just nonsense. My wife was convinced that Hitler was guided and led by an invisible spirit.[66]

If it must happen, then let it happen as fast as possible. Do you understand these are words from the Avatāra, from God? What can we make of them? The fortuneteller "saw blood, misery, distress, chaos and a cruel demise" — her prediction came true, but it is not complete. In its churning, the sky changed from yellow to red, then black — the colors of the Weimar Republic and postwar Germany. She saw the devastation of the war-torn Reich; but she also saw the ruin a Judeo-Allied victory wrought.

Let us further the fortune: the future holds *blood, misery, distress, chaos,* and a *cruel demise!* How will you face such a future?

Will you fold under the heavy burden, or will you relish the chance to prove your worth to Almighty God? There is no escaping the destined future; you must, if you are to prove your worth to God and folk, meet your fate head on — *Optimism is cowardice; only dreamers believe in ways out!* You must *long for nothing more ardently* than to return again to this same life, under the same circumstances, *for all time.*⁶⁷ This is the philosophy of *nonetheless!* This is Hitlerist accelerationism! *Let it happen as fast as possible!* Accelerate the end of this greatest of evils — the power of the satanic Jew. This is what it means to be an honorable and loyal Aryan.

And politics? — In this time of the Innocent Jew, politics, at best, is optimistic cowardice! Leave your fear behind, Aryan; instead, churn the calm skies, tumble and thunder the menacing madness of an architect. Your design is the end of linearity, which bodes the end of its imposers; your design is the gnashing of teeth and the cursing of the demon that condemns you to this Eternal Return; your design is the love of fate — *amor fati* — that promises your escape into the halls of Valhalla.

But it is no *escape* — it is rather an *embrace* stronger than any preceding it. It is escape through a severe acceptance, an acceptance *nonetheless*. Does the Jew wish to enslave? Then you, Aryan, will be the omnipresent, invisible *serf*. You will be the *warrior in the shadows* the Jew departs to wreak havoc in the daylight; you will be the *forgotten one* who works the humble, but *all-too-important* tasks for the tyrannizing Jew; and from your hands falls *the greatest weight* — the weight which crushes the one who threatens Nature and all who faithfully protect her. The Jew wants to win, to *dominate*; Aryan, *you will help it win*, wittingly, and on God's terms. You are the knowing thrall, the invisible god.

Victory for the Jew is destruction, and Shiva emerges from the fall of the greatest weight.

13.

Only those who die fighting the Enemy, the Fenrir Wolf, with full awareness of the combat, confronting death like an Initiation [will be immortalized]. [This is] the Initiation of Esoteric Hitlerism. For this there are fixed numbers. Today, the doors of Valhalla are almost closed. Only 108 more Heroes will be able to enter. They are the *Einherier*.⁶⁸

So wrote Serrano. The *Einherjar* — heroes of old and new, fighting simultaneously for Wotan, the *Allvater*, the *Avatāra* — emerge from the shadows. They are the *Ein-Herjar*, the *lone warriors* who choose (in the words of Tacitus) "dark nights to fight, and by means of the terror and shadow of a ghostly army they cause panic, since no enemy can bear a sight so unexpected and hellish..."⁶⁹

Of those remaining able to enter Valhalla, the *figure* is 108; the *figurative* is only fixed. Numbers, if misunderstood, can be deceptions. Time is both waning and infinite — but the number has always been set: few places remain to be filled in the Valhalla of Allvater.

Will you earn a place at the sacred table, at the side of those who have fought, will fight, and fight still with honor and loyalty in the Cosmic Struggle? Few spots remain. One must be truly great to earn something so rare, so near to God.

Ein-Herjar — the *solitary fighter*, bold and unrelenting. Spengler understood this well:

> The genuine human soul now forms — a very solitary soul ... with the proud and pensive look of one knowing his own destiny, with unrestrained sense of power in the fist habituated to deeds, a foe to everyone, killing, *hating*, resolute to conquer or die. This soul is profounder and more passionate than that of any animal whatsoever. It stands in irreconcilable opposition to the whole world...⁷⁰

The meaning of "the whole world" now is clear: it is the Judeo-system that dominates and subjugates Nature and her defenders; it is the Judeo-system that rules through fear and shame, relegating *freedom* to mere slogan and euphemism for *tyranny*; it is the enormity of the Judeo-system encompassing the vast, imposed space of the senses. Only the bold and unrelenting — those who fight *nonetheless* — can ever hope to confront such evil.

The world trembles when the Aryan recognizes what *true freedom* — that is, what *necessity* — is.[71]

The Figurative World — Notes

1. See Immanuel Kant, *Critique of Pure Reason*, "Transcendental Doctrine of Judgment."
2. See Friedrich, *Hitler Avatāra* (2023) for an in-depth study of the topic.
3. Richard Wagner, *Deutsche Kunst und Deutsche Politik*.
4. This was Albert Einstein's infamous quip on quantum entanglement, reflecting his dissatisfaction and demand for "local reality."
5. See Henry Bellows for more on the Heimdall-Wotan overlap; *Poetic Edda* (1936), 165.
6. Søren Kierkegaard, *Philosophical Fragments* (1987), "The Absolute Paradox" and *Training in Christianity* (2004), 58.
7. See *Hitler Avatāra* for a study of *faith* and *contemporaneousness*.
8. *The Upanishads* (1965), Prasna Upanishad, 68.
9. *Poetic Edda*, "Hovamal," §155.
10. *Hitler Avatāra*, 57.
11. *Poetic Edda*, "Grimnismol," §23.
12. See Friedrich, *Myth and Sun: Essays of the ARCHETYPE* (2022) for more on the *Führerprinzip*.
13. Lisa Pine, "The NS-Ordensburgen: training for political leadership," *History of Education* (2014), vol. 43, no. 2, 233-234.
14. Miguel Serrano, *Adolf Hitler: The Ultimate Avatar* (2014), 323.
15. Waiblinger, 'Ein Jahr Ordensburg: Ausblick,' *Der Orden: Blätter der Ordensburg Vogelsang*, 1:4; emphasis added.
16. Artemy Magun, "Karl Marx and Hannah Arendt on the Jewish Question: Political Theology as a Critique," *Continental Philosophy Review* 45, no. 4 (12, 2012), 552.
17. Ludwig Feuerbach, *The Essence of Christianity* (2008).
18. Karl Marx, "On the Jewish Question" (1844).
19. Karl Marx, "On the Jewish Question." See also Nietzsche (*Antichrist*, §24): "Jews are the most *fateful* people in the history of the world: their influence has so falsified the reasoning of mankind in this matter that today the Christian can cherish anti-Semitism without realizing that it is no more than the *final consequence of Judaism*."
20. Judges 8:24-27 (NIV).
21. Buber, *Kingship of God* (1967), 63.
22. Bhagavad Gita, IV.21, translated by A.C. Bhaktivedanta Swami Prabhupada (all Gita translations are his unless otherwise noted).
23. Bhagavad Gita, VII.16-17.
24. *Poetic Edda*, "Guthrunarkvitha," §20.
25. *Poetic Edda*, "Fra Dautha Sinfjotla," introductory note.

[26] *Bundesarchiv Berlin NS* 22/27 (18 January 1941), "Über personelle Auswertung der Schulung zur Personalpolitik," 3-4.
[27] See *Myth and Sun* for more on the healthy self and society.
[28] *Der Spiegel* interview (1966).
[29] Serrano, *Adolf Hitler*, 87; minor edits for readability.
[30] *The Wall Street Journal* (WSJ), the second-largest newspaper in the United States, is owned by News Corp, which has arch-Zionist Rupert Murdoch as its executive chairman. The WSJ's publisher is the likely Jew Almar Latour (married Abby Schmelz). This particular article was highlighted and positively discussed by MSNBC after its publication (31 October 2023). MSNBC is owned by Comcast, which has Jew Brian Roberts as chairman and CEO. MSNBC's parent company is NBCUniversal Media Group, which has Jew Mark Lazarus as chairman. NBCUniversal Media Group's parent company is NBCUniversal, which has Jew Bonnie Hammer as vice-chairman; Hammer has earned several awards from various Jewish organizations (e.g., B'nai B'rith and the ADL) for her work promoting the Jewish race and combatting "hate."

This article, just one among many like it, and its circulation illustrate the fabricated nature of the divide between "left" (MSNBC) and "right" (WSJ) media. As always in media, when Jews and Israel are "at stake," all march to the same tune: protect the sacred Jews at all costs; defame detractors; fight for Jewish dominion. The same "divide" evaporates in governments across the West when Israel is up for discussion. Only outlier, low-ranking MPs or congresspersons — who are firm Marxists — have actual hostility toward Israel. And it is these same Marxists in academia, with their rejection of blind calls to "support Israel," who have now raised the ire of the Jewish media. Further muddling the ostensible dichotomy is the fact that most, if not all, leftists (Marxists) are only hostile toward Israel because they believe Jews are "white" — and their support for Palestine is another white-versus-nonwhite banner behind which to march; that is, it is only another opportunity to express their hatred for white people. Of course, this anti-white hate is fomented by both media and academia — each of which is the nearly exclusive domain of Jews and Marxists.

This, in turn, illustrates the parasitical, destructive nature of the Judeo-system. The children of the Judeo-system (leftist academicians) attempt to devour their ideological parents (Jews); the Jews, of course, will win by pummeling "rogue" professors or colleges in the media, but the leftist academicians will, despite ambiguous allegiance to the Jews, largely, nevertheless be left to pollute the minds of future students. Likewise, the anti-white politicians will be left in office and will continue to receive campaign donations from supportive Jews (or their surrogates). For the Judeo-system, foremost, must eradicate all remnants of Aryan lifeways. This, in part, is done by university indoctrination and governmental policy.

Less than a week (02 November 2023) after the WSJ published "The Global War on Jews," it ran another op-ed entitled "Israel Needs a New Leader," in which an attempt is made to deflect the stain of the Jews onto Israel's Netanyahu. MSNBC again picked up the discussion, advocating for a similar conclusion. In the wake of still more extremist action from Israel, many of the most ardent supporters are scrambling to lay the blame on an "outlier" — but certainly not Israel and definitely not the Jews. The masses, naturally, will take the bait.

Hillary Clinton, meanwhile, is invoked across many media platforms as some kind of seer for her 2016 presidential-debate remarks about Israel and Hamas. Few bother to consider the context that, as Secretary of State, she was *instrumental* in *fomenting* the very instability (in both the Mideast and North Africa) she "predicts." This is not to mention the fact that the United States, as surrogate for Jews and Trotskyites, has provoked instability the world over since at least World War I, *causing the very problems it pretends to solve* (a Jewish trait).

[31] DeWitt H. Parker, *Schopenhauer Selections* (1928), xxi.
[32] Nietzsche, *The Will to Power*, §1067.
[33] Carl Jung, *The Archetypes and the Collective Unconscious* (1969), 4. εἶδος or *idea, form.*
[34] Jung, *The Archetypes*, 13.
[35] "When we lose, we can of course hope that somehow the gods or 'history' will turn our defeats into conditions for future victories. But in the end, we can only win by winning" (Greg Johnson, "Against Accelerationism" [Counter Currents, 06 January 2020]).
[36] Jung, *The Archetypes*, 20.
[37] See Miguel Serrano, *Manu: For the Man to Come*, "My Disenchantment with Carl Gustav Jung."
[38] *Hitler Avatāra*, 69.
[39] *Hitler Avatāra*, 85.
[40] Homer, *Iliad*, Book XI.
[41] Dares the Phrygian, *The Trojan War* (1966), 143.
[42] Tacitus, *Complete Works of Tacitus* (1942), *Germania*: 43, 730.
[43] Cf. "Population and Technics" above.
[44] Serrano also chronicles the Judaizing of the majority-European South American countries in his *The Golden Thread, Adolf Hitler: The Ultimate Avatar*, and *Manu: For the Man to Come*.

45 When outright fear is not pursued, *shame*, its precursor, is. Shame is meant to be elicited from the fear-for-the-Jew stories; this shame is always tied to a more expansive fear for livelihood.
46 Serrano, *Manu*, 73.
47 Deuteronomy 2:25 (NIV).
48 Deuteronomy 7:2, 5-6 (NIV), via Moses.
49 Serrano, *Manu*, 193.
50 Preceding quotes from Serrano, *Manu*, 195, 196; emphasis added. Cf. *The Ultimate Avatar*, 827: "These dark hypnotic waves are projected from the World Center of Black Magic in Jerusalem."
51 Serrano, *Adolf Hitler*, 833; emphasis added.
52 Jung, *The Archetypes*, 23.
53 Serrano, *Adolf Hitler*, 127.
54 Serrano, *Adolf Hitler*, 126.
55 Benton Bradberry, *The Myth of German Villainy* (2012), 98-99; citing Vladimir Soloukhin's *The Bloodlust of Bolshevism*.
56 Jung, *The Archetypes*, 13.
57 Jung, *The Archetypes*, 31.
58 Adolf Hitler, 08 November 1940 (speech).
59 Adolf Hitler, 12 February 1936 (speech). See T. Dalton's *Hitler on the Jews* (2019) for extended passages.
60 Or *faith of the noble (Aryan)*: आर्यस्य श्रद्धा (*āryasya śraddhā*).
61 "The Good is that which transcends and uplifts; it is sacrificing oneself for the benefit of the whole that reflects oneself; this reflection is physical, mental, and spiritual; the Good is *one thing*. Purity of heart is to will one thing" (*Hitler Avatāra*, 85).
62 Anna Plaim, *Living with Hitler* (2018), 193.
63 Hesiod, *Works and Days* (1914), lines 174-201; translation modified for readability. Cf. Bhagavad Gita, I.41-43 and *Poetic Edda*, "Voluspo."
64 Nietzsche, *Joyful Wisdom*, §283.
65 Bhagavad Gita, VIII.7.
66 Herman Döhring, *Living with Hitler* (2018), 137.
67 Nietzsche, *Joyful Wisdom*, §341.
68 Serrano, *Adolf Hitler*, 377-378.
69 Andy Orchard, *Dictionary of Norse Myth and Legend* (1997), 36 — quoting Tacitus' *Germania*; the same passage can also be found here: *Complete Works of Tacitus* (1942), 730.
70 Oswald Spengler, *Man and Technics* (1963), 42.
71 Cf. Jünger, *The Worker* (2017), §1.

Afterword

With diviner features doth it now arise, seducing by its suffering; and verily! it will yet thank you for o'erthrowing it, ye subverters!

— Friedrich Nietzsche
Thus Spoke Zarathustra

The deepest happiness of man lies in the fact that he will be sacrificed and the highest art of command consists in the capacity to present goals that are worthy of sacrifice.

— Ernst Jünger

1.

In the end was the Word, and the Word was with God, and the Word was God. The Avatāra speaks the Word. Adherents hear the Word and obey; to obey is to fight. *Nonetheless*.

It has been said that we fight for the MAN TO COME. This means we fight to end the time that fixes us to a technicized and exploitative existence; it means we fight against the life of the miscreants who deserve grim consequences for their godless actions; it means we fight against the Jew and its Electric Messiah. The struggle for a reorientation to God and Nature is against *time* and even *life*[1] itself, but it must be waged nonetheless. *The Hitlerist fights for what is right in the face of insurmountable odds — not for material gain, but for communion and reconciliation with God.*

What follows in Shiva's wake? This is neither for us to decide, nor is it our concern. With the advent of Kalki we will know our actions to be right. But *what if*, Aryan — what if Kalki is not some *future* figure for whom we pave the way, but is instead those remaining few who hold fast to the Idea? *The Einherjar*. In this world of disappearing people, only the *faithful, who fight with open eyes, warriors in the shadows, agents of divine light* — only they are bearers of the Word. This Word does not come to set nonexistent *humanity* free, but Nature. This Word is the destroyer of the Judeo-system, that enslaver and degrader of life. This Word is life *indeed*, and in *deed* it stifles the Breathing Hate; in *truth* it removes the Organic Lie.

The deed is clear, but *what is truth?* Pilate put this question to the King of the Jews[2]; the answer was a revaluation of all values that assailed the Aryans' Achilles heel *for all time*. No longer did the Aryan sacrifice for his folk; Europe's penchant for spiritual-cultural elevation through sacrifice was now exploited by Judeo-Christianity and shifted to popery and a Jewish chimera. The Aryan's eyes were diverted to heaven while Jewish schemes snatched his soul. But a new Word is destined to reclaim Aryan attention.

This Word as deed is less *paradox* than *heterodox* — it is *rebellion* against a system that subdues and demeans all passionate expressions of will, it is *rebellion* against a system that plots for an anthill of tenant-drones goaded and galvanized through permanent pulses of fear and shame. This Word is the *triumph of the will*, and it has already won — because it *is* one: *Ein. Ein-Herjar*: the *one* of the North, that "region of the sun ... [and] land of immortality where there is no fear"[3]; the *one* that transcends time because it perceives with the eye that sees even in the dark; the *one* that battles in this Cosmic Struggle *through all time*, because time itself is a figment of perception reinforced within the Judeo-system.

Few places remain in the Valhalla of Allvater-Avatāra — they remain, but they are filled *nonetheless*. Each Aryan knows, in *deed* and *truth*, whether his place is secured. There exists but one army in one time; the MAN TO COME is the MAN WHO WAS and the MAN WHO IS. Kalki is *you*, spread among the nations-become-states, scattered across time and within it, inserted into Judeo linearity for one divine purpose. Your deed and truth — is Kalki's.

Your work is to fight *nonetheless*.

Your salvation is Nature's defense.

2.

The ninth Avatāra of God chose to manifest in what became the German Reich because it was at the heart of Europe, the nascent dominion of the Jew. Adolf Hitler appeared in the heart of Europe because he was the culmination of a collective frustration.

After the collapse of *Simulacrum Romae* — the former Aryan-Roman *imperium* that degenerated into a Semiticized *empire* — what would become Germany, the heart of Europe, the same folk who drove the final stake into zombified Rome, became world-bearer of the Aryan soul. It is often quipped that the Holy Roman Empire was not *holy*, *Roman*, or *empire*; but this is false. The First Reich bore the greatest weight, the stamp of Imperium, to mark a millennium; this was its *holy* mission. However, this Reich succumbed to the Semiticized drama, the linearity of the illusion, and could not therefore elevate Imperium to its deserved heights; its materiality, then, made it both *Roman* and a wallower in *empire*.

Largely excluded from the Germanic Imperium, Britannia, Iberia-Gaul, and Russia settled into their imperialistic impulses; their sediment was rich soil for Ahasuerus, the itinerant Jew in search of a new host. England became, as Serrano held, the land of "Aryan bodies and Jew souls"[4]; Iberia-Gaul became the land of the internationalist *lingua Franca* and the Sephardim; Russia and her western reaches became incubator of the Ashkenazim. The inner tumult of the First Reich, meanwhile, kept the Jew on the periphery.[5]

Sturm und Drang characterized Germania — to the point of nonexistence. How could it exist when its focus was divine Imperium? Germania was an assembly of absolutists, each with their own duty to an inner faith; it was a fledgling-nation of warrior-priests, all taking flight in opposing directions. And while Germania developed spiritually, its Jew-infested borderlands grew materially. England, France, Spain, and Russia all became imperialistic powers. From among them, only Napoleon saw beyond mere money to the nonexistence of divine Imperium. Glory was his philter for God, but he was not German; he did not rage with the faith of a spiritual creator, and in the end, his eye for material-grandeur evinced Mediterranean origins. Two forces, ultimately, finished the Napoleonic mission: materiality and spirituality. On the one hand, England, Russia, and internationalist powers in France rose like antibodies against the virus threatening their imperialistic ambitions; on the other hand, Prussian pride, itself feeling the pull of past and future Reichs — an unarticulated struggle against time —, could not submit to western invaders.

The same *Sturm und Drang* that undermined the material ambitions of nonexistent Germania and Napoleonic creep found expression in the Romantic Movement preceding the rise of the Second and Third Reichs. Romanticism, in its love for individual expression of the collective spiritual will and hearkening back to a primordial soul, is often derided by worldly materialists[6]: Romantics are only idealistic dreamers; rationalistic materialists, on the other hand, are shrewd opportunists — this is the general assessment. Romanticism was not an expression of idlers, however, but the swell of faith sown in the heart of Germania; it was the *Sturm und Drang* loosing the vice of materiality; it was a fight *against time*.

The Germanic will, the spiritual-cultural urge of the Aryan, is ever an embrace of the spirit animating time; but this spirit, this *Geist*, is unbound by time. The *Zeitgeist* is not an emergent spirit *of* the age, but the inborn spirit *animating* the age, and this concept could only ever be expressed in the Romantic, nonexistent cultural-soul of Germania. *Zeitgeist* is the reverberation of revolution — this is its proper meaning. Judeo-time is tyranny in liberal dress; it is every movement that is with time. No liberal revolution could bear the Germanic *Zeitgeist*, for a *Zeitgeist* is *against* time and bears the inborn freedom of the Supreme Creator. Liberal revolutions, which only ever reflect the spirit *of* the age, are manufactured imitations birthed in the mind of the Jew; liberal revolutions are populations wielded as implements, population as technics. Liberal revolutions are not revolutions at all, but only *ensnarements*.[7] The spirit *animating* the age is not *of* the age; it is neither canny nor rational; it is boundless and brimming with life — the life of a Creator. Romanticism, then, was *not* reactionary, just as faith is not reactionary. Faith, by any name, is a *revolution* against time.[8]

Aryan faith is not about any romantic longing for the past, just as accelerationism is not about the absurd push to rebuild society "for the white man." Rather, both seek an understanding of the life-giving force of a spirit-culture and strive to defend it. To defend the boundless spirit animating time means to revolt against the time imposed upon reality by materiality. To fight for God means to fight for the end of the system that denies God. The only expression of Aryan faith, which has remained consistent throughout the existence of nonexistent Germania in this Kali-Yuga, is the defense of Nature. It is not, nor ever was, an anachronistic longing for an idyllic past; rather, it is, was, and will be a Cosmic Struggle for the soul of creation through boundless time. The Aryan defense of Nature is misinterpreted as "romantic" or "backwards" because it is forever *against time*; it is the fight *for* infinite time *against* Jewish imposition. The defense of Nature is necessarily against "the Enlightenment, modern science, liberalism, the market, Marxism, and the Jews"[9] — because all are expressions of the Judeo-system, which is born of the Lord of Darkness.

Hitlerism is this defense of Nature, for the unfolding of Nature has been frustrated by the Jew and its Judeo-system time and again. The Jew cannot do otherwise than thwart the creation of the Supreme Creator, for the Jew is a fabrication and imitation of the very creation it hates. *The Jew will never be good* — which is to say, the Jew will never act in accordance with Nature, the Jew will never stop meddling in the affairs of others (despite its constant calls for "self-determination"), and the Jew will never stop working toward its supremacy at the expense of all Gentiles. The Jew is the Breathing Hate, the Organic Lie, the Personification of Innocence masking the Eternal Enemy and Planetary Murderer. Adolf Hitler unmasked the Jew *for all time*. The Aryan, whose will culminated in the existence of Hitler Avatāra, has as his duty the sacrifice for which the Führer provided the command.

There exists a dream whose sleep is not yet slept. In this round of the Eternal Return, sleep finds us all.

3.

Dreamless sleep haunts us. Our inner world has been turned outward. We visit the void in our sleep because, inwardly, we are void. The water of soul rushing by in our night excursions has turned to vacuum: a thing that *is* by not being. We look outward and are pleased with our status and shimmer; the inner world, if acknowledged at all, repels us. We are terrified of knowing ourselves but fizz over the fear machines in our homes, hands, and pockets. We imagine the chaos of Kronos is natural, as long as the belly is full. And if it's not full? Well, there is *always next time*.

Always — next — time — and the snare tightens.

We discuss the last election. We see recent changes, shake our head, and kick at the dirt. *It could have been different*, we say to our friend, *if only ... if only*. We think that all this change is so very new and surely wouldn't have happened if the other party had been elected. We see meaning in the signs and symbols of our oppression; we pay homage to this oppression. We believe in our comfort. *It could be worse!* But the worst is yet to come. Listen to Jung:

> The growing impoverishment of symbols has a meaning. It is a development that has an inner consistency. Everything that we have not thought about, and that has therefore been deprived of a meaningful connection with our developing consciousness, has got lost.[10]

Meaning was lost on the conveyor belt of time — a belt that brands us with ritualistic sixes, consumes our blood and being, and moves us closer to the satanic gullet. *Fear, Nazis, Holocaust; fear, antisemitism, barbarity; fear, Israel, disaster* — keep silent, Gentile: know your place, not yourself. Crisis after crisis, disaster after disaster: On the belt rolls, charged and spun by the Electric Messiah. Disaster, *dis-astro*, the ill-starred event, the negation of the sun — this is the webbed veil obscuring the Third Eye. The "inner consistency" of the Electric Messiah is deceit, and deceit will not cease until we see beyond the veil. The Swastika is the sign of the sun; the Judeo-system presses hard to negate the sun with the veil of *disaster*.

Your duty is clear, Aryan: fight for the revelation of the sun; fight for the Avatāra; fight for the expression of your will the disasters of the Jew bury under the ant-heap of time. Your will is Kalki, the Avatāra manifested beyond space and time; you are the "spooky action at a distance" the faithless will never comprehend; you are the invisible god defending Nature with a shield bearing the *Hakenkreuz*, the revolving rays of the shining sun; you part the veil with divine light. Kalki is the *Lichtbringer* who dispels — *for all time* — the billowing tyranny of the Lord of Darkness.

You are filled with the hope only the faithful can have. But it is not a selfish hope. The light beyond the darkness belongs to the Black Sun, and this Sun demands sacrifice — the same sacrifice the Avatāra demands of itself. Billows on the horizon bear an ill omen: *ill* for the Aryan because his subjugation is just beginning; *ill* for the

Jew because it knows the end draws nigh. The climactic event ushering ill in the Cosmic Struggle is *apocalypse*; there is no saving our world. Destiny for all is total devastation; and from the wreckage arises — the demon's blank stare.

But *your duty*, Aryan — *your duty* will be complete. Perhaps, then, one day in the distant past, unimaginable future, or ever-wheeling present, the honor and loyalty that marked your life and crowned your end will cleave the void. And from this space, time itself will cease, marking the end of the Judeo-system — *for all time*.

> *With diviner features doth it now arise,*
> *seducing by its suffering;*
> *and verily! it will yet thank you for...*
> *its arrival quickly ushering.*

4.

The *metaprophecy*:

> As Napoleon Bonaparte sat in St. Helena, miserable and demoralized, he wrote the following prophetic words: *I failed. I was not strong enough to unify Europe. But someone will come after me who will raise my banner once more, and finish my work, and then no one will speak of England any longer, but rather one will speak of a Napoleon.*
>
> These prophetic words of Napoleon Bonaparte, England's sworn enemy, are now being fulfilled. European unity is being forged now that the Jew has been driven from it. Under the leadership of its Führer Adolf Hitler, Germany will carry the banner of this ancient, yet ever young, part of the earth. *At the end of this war, Germany will win and Europe will be united!*[11]

Robert Ley made this prophecy in 1944, little more than a year before he ended his turn in the *time-that-wheels-in-all-directions*. It could only have meaning today if there is victory in defeat. Such a victory is one of spirit, one of the Idea. There are those yet faithful to the Idea; the Judeo-Allies did not exterminate or "de-Nazify" all of them, though they tried. Material victory was and is impossible. We honor our predecessors for their inspiring work, but they were, as are all of us, subject to Providence.

Reflect on all those who "failed" to achieve material victory. The "traditionalists" and "ethnocentrists" cannot begin to approach the tracks these giants have left in the muck of materiality. Spiritual victory, the sole enduring victory, can only be won through fanatical dedication to the Idea. All else is snare for corruption. In seeking material defeat for those belonging to the Judeo-system, the Hitlerist does not, in turn, seek material victory. The material defeat of the Enemy is, instead, one aspect of Hitlerist Imperium, one aspect of spiritual necessity and triumph. Rejection of material victory is the patent rejection of the materialists' cause. It is rejection of the Jewish Imperium.

Faith and deed are the two facets of Hitlerist Imperium. This acknowledges Providence, which human beings cannot deny.[12] "All human labors are doomed to fail if they are not blessed by the light of Providence."[13] In this Kali-Yuga there can be no more material victory for the forces of light; this age is ruled by shadow. The work of the Hitlerist is to dispel the shadow. Dispel the shadow of your soul through faith; dispel the darkness of the Judeo-system through your struggle against it.

Adolf Hitler's mission was to unmask the Jew; in this, he succeeded. His victory is ours and presents us with our mission: bring about the end of the Judeo-system. With or without us it will end; but our duty is to fight for the righteousness our Creator demands.

5.

History is not ended. It will sooner or later take up the threads apparently broken off forever and knit them together in a new pattern.
— Rudolf Hess, from a 1945 letter to his wife

Rudolf Hess was prisoner of the Jews and their Allies for *forty-six* years in Spandau Prison following the Nuremberg show-trials; twenty of those years he spent in solitary confinement, the lone inmate in a 600-bed prison. Hess was murdered in the prison yard's recreational garden on 17 August 1987, aged 93. Despite the Judeo-system's obsessive and vengeful attempt to erase Hess' sacrifice, his spirit endures in the soul of the remaining fighters.

Rudolf Hess was a martyr for peace and the future of Europe. He left his wife and young son, abandoned the comfort of his post and the relative security of the Reich, and forfeited his future for the possibility of a lasting place for the Germanic folk among the peoples of this world. Hess was neither a criminal nor a terrorist. He was a good man who fought heroically in the Great War, continued his fight against the alien forces threatening his people after the war, and ultimately sacrificed everything he loved for the chance to stop the Judeo-menace that, if victorious, promised an end to Aryan culture as it was yet known. Rudolf Hess is a hero for his efforts and was martyred for his actions.

On 10 May 1941, nearly at the peak of Germany's power, the onetime deputy and adjutant under Adolf Hitler flew to Scotland in a bold attempt to secure peace in the west, thereby preserving Germanic stock in Europe and the Americas and freeing Germany's hand to defend Europe's future against the Judeo-Marxist horde that was soon to strike. The Soviets were arraying forces on the Reich's eastern border, intent on securing more European territory at the expense of a beleaguered Germany fighting yet another two-front war.

Not a week before Hess' flight, Stalin and other senior officials were celebrating a commissioning of military officers; as banquet turned to bash, Stalin announced that all territory which could be attained diplomatically had been already, boasting that an aggressive war against Germany was imminent. This news was quickly leaked to the Reich and was confirmed with separate interrogations of two Soviet generals after the war's eastern outbreak.[14] Knowing that the Ribbentrop-Molotov nonaggression pact meant nothing more than a stall for time to either side, the time to act was now: if Germany remained idle, it would lose the initiative. While hoping for peace, Hitler prepared for war[15] — the two-front war he decried. A daring, stealthy plan was made — one that would, if successful, *secure the hope*: Hess, acting as Reich emissary, would make the solo flight to Scotland and meet with the conservative Duke of Hamilton who would galvanize a governmental coalition to thwart

Churchill and settle peace with Germany; this would prevent the war that destined the destruction of a Germanic, European future. This plan, for which Hess seemed suited — fiercely loyal to Führer and folk as he was, senior-ranking, and a capable pilot —, was hastily devised to allow for maximum probability of success and, should it fail, deniability. Hess would never betray Hitler's confidence if things went awry, nor would Hess take offense at being labeled "mad" if the Reich needed to distance itself from its final means of securing peace in the west.

Rudolf Hess embodied the Germanic sense of sacrifice, and for this we honor his memory. Despite the Judeo-system's most fervent contrariwise efforts, Hess defied Jewish vengeance, kept his honor, and remained loyal to Führer and folk to the very end.

"The very existence of Hess is a reminder that Britain, not Germany, wanted a global war and massive loss of life," M. Raphael Johnson wrote in 2001,

> Hess reminds the world that peace overtures came from National Socialists, not the English ruling class. The entire mythology of World War II might come crumbling down with the release of Hess and any sort of popular interest in his story. For, most certainly, politics in the early 21st century are still highly conditioned by the myths of World War II. Without them, the system loses its legitimacy.[16]

One would think the Judeo-system *would* lose legitimacy, but it is not meant to be. Sign after sign points to the evil of the Jews, their Judeo-bots, and the criminal illusion of the Judeo-system — but the masses seek sanctuary under the dank Jewish membrane nevertheless. Proofs can only bring one to the brink, but the leap remains an *individual decision*[17]; yet in this time of *disappearing people*, most *do not have the aptitude to make individual decisions*. This is the result of Jewry's *mass Phobos-hypnosis* — fueled by toxic foods, chemical drinks, stupefying pharmaceuticals, media droning, and indoctrinatory education. Aryans must stop thinking about "normal" solutions to "normal" problems. *Normalcy* is part of the Judeo-illusion, which is why it is so often *trans*-formed and re-*enforced* through *Phobos-hypnosis*. The more *fanatical* your actions in defiance of the Judeo-system and in defense of Nature, the more righteous is your life and legacy. The Aryan is confronted with a Jewish supremacy shouldered by proto-zombies steeped in an illusion: *normal solutions are for slaves and extinction*.

Rudolf Hess lived a fanatical life and defied the consequences. He is an inspiration to all remaining Aryans. His existence was an affront to the sordid Judeo-system, which is why they kept his absurd imprisonment quiet and even more quietly murdered him.[18]

No matter what the Judeo-system does, however, it cannot erase its own stain. It cannot erase, for instance, that the preeminent Judeo-hero Winston Churchill was financially backed by the Focus for the Defense of Freedom and Peace group. The *Focus Group*, as it was called, was an ultra-liberal and anti-German political action committee, mainly funded by the Jew Robert Cohen, with the tacit objective of inducing war with Germany and ousting Hitler from power. They saw financing the notoriously hawkish Churchill as their principal means of doing this, making him essentially a shill for Anglo-Judeo money interests. The Judeo-system cannot delete the fact that Churchill spent more than the equivalent of £50,000 a year on alcohol and had a £54,000 holiday-gambling habit, and that by 1938 he was more than £2 million in debt. The system cannot gloss over or dismiss as "propaganda" — *no matter how hard it tries* — the simple truth that Churchill was so indebted because of frivolous spending and back taxes that he had to be bailed out: the Austrian-born Jew Henry Strakosch — banker, businessman, and chairman of *The Economist* — cleared Churchill's debt on multiple occasions, totaling nearly £1 million during his lifetime; upon his death, Strakosch bequeathed another £1 million to Churchill and canceled a sizable loan in 1943. Strakosch considered Churchill to be Judaized-Britain's only chance to frustrate the ascent of Hitler's Third Reich.[19]

The Judeo-system cannot expunge from history that no world leader attempted to secure peace, before or during the war, more than Adolf Hitler. Hitler made a number of overtures to the Brits and Poles to reconcile the Versailles-imposed injustice of (1) the forced dislocation of German-born Poles (and their subsequent persecution in Poland, and (2) the non-existent Danzig corridor, linking the German Reich with its major port city. Defying sensibility, the Poles rejected all compromise with Germany, instead counting on Britain to defend its anti-German aim. Britain, despite being overwhelmingly resource- and population-rich because of its imperialistic obsession, firmly rejected the possibility of a powerful Germany to contend with on the Continent, and instead vied for continued European and imperial-colonial dominance shared between it and France, which itself had substantial colonial holdings; for this, they turned a local war between Germany and Poland into a global war in service to the Jewish Imperium: annihilation of Aryan lifeways and destruction of dignity *at all cost*.

No, the Jews and their system cannot erase their stain; but it is their destiny, their archetype, to try nevertheless. After Hess' death, Spandau Prison was demolished and a shopping mall was erected in its place. Thus, another obligation of the Jewish World Order — placing its valueless stamp on any shred of humanity and distracting its Judeo-bot citizens into oblivion — was fulfilled.

6.

Rudolf Hess was ahead of his time, for he was fanatical in times of plenty. His words and actions, inspired by Hitler Avatāra, spoke to the sacrifice necessary in the Cosmic Struggle. He saw the necessity of combat despite imagined success; he ascended against time, he endured beyond time; and in his death, he fulfilled the archetype of both his folk and their Eternal Enemy. Hero Hess obliterated the *wheel of dharma*. If Hess-the-man has been freed from the Eternal Return because of his heroism and undying loyalty, his spirit will abide in subsequent rounds. A future *bodhisattva* of the ancient past will embody this spirit and liberate his folk from demiurgical bondage.

This time the ignoble Judeo-system will be broken.
This time the miscreants will wash in righteous vengeance.
This time Nature will triumph — for Nature cannot do otherwise.

Victory is Shiva and Shiva is Victory. *Sieg Heil!*

Afterword — Notes

[1] That is, the Judaized life of the Judeo-system.
[2] John 18:38.
[3] *The Upanishads* (1965), Prasna Upanishad, 68.
[4] Miguel Serrano, *Adolf Hitler: The Ultimate Avatar* (2014), 800.
[5] "Liberalism provided the battering ram for the Jews to enter public life in Western civilization. Thanks to the revolts against the traditional order, the Jewish speculator and moneychanger became dominant over Europe.... Later in the nineteenth century, Jews were able to enter the USA without the burden of that Tradition which they sought to destroy in Europe... This culminated in 1933 with the assumption to the presidency of [FDR and his retinue of Jewish advisors: Samuel Rosenman, Felix Frankfurter, Louis Brandeis, and James Warburg]" (Kerry Bolton, *Yockey* [2018], 135).
[6] See, for instance, Jeffrey Herf's *Reactionary Modernism: Technology, Culture, and Politics in Weimar and the Third Reich* (1990). "Reactionary Modernism" is only contemporary verbiage for the manifestation of the spiritual-cultural thread tying all exhibitions of Germanic faith together.
[7] All "revolutions" in the Kali-Yuga, since the departure of the Avatāra in 1945, are fated to be mere liberal imitations — even the most "conservative" "revolution."
[8] One cannot but be reminded of Ayatollah Khomeini's words on Islam: "Islam is the religion of *militant individuals* who are *committed to truth and justice*. It is the religion of those who *desire freedom and independence*. It is the school of those who *struggle against imperialism*. But the servants of imperialism have ... created in men's minds a false notion of Islam. The defective version of Islam ... is intended to deprive Islam of its vital, *revolutionary* aspect ... and allow them to live lives worthy of human beings" (*Islamic Government: Governance of the Jurist*, translated by H. Algar).
[9] Herf, *Reactionary Modernism*, 5. The fight against "modern science" is none other than the fight against the apotheosization of science. *Science-as-tool* — i.e., the intended use of science — is not rejected.
[10] Carl Jung, *The Archetypes and the Collective Unconscious* (1969), 14.
[11] Robert Ley, *Pesthauch der Welt* (1944).
[12] Adolf Hitler, 30 January 1933 (speech).
[13] Adolf Hitler, 01 May 1933 (speech).
[14] Wayland D. Smith, reviewing *Failure at Nuremberg*: http://www.ihr.org/jhr/v04/v04p119_Smith.html.

[15] Adolf Hitler, *Second Book*, ch. 3: "Preparation for war was never the task of any truly great statesmen, but rather the inner and thorough training of a people, so its future could be secured almost as by law…"
[16] M. Raphael Johnson, *The Barnes Review* (July/August 2001), "The Tragedy of Rudolf Hess: What Kind of Man was He?"
[17] Friedrich, *Hitler Avatāra* (2023), 69.
[18] See Abdallah Melaouhi's *Rudolf Hess: His Murder and Betrayal* (2013), W. Hugh Thomas' *The Murder of Rudolf Hess* (1979), and Wolf Rüdiger Hess' *My Father Rudolf Hess* (1987) for an introduction to the deception surrounding the sanctioned story of Hess' demise.
[19] David Lough, *No More Champagne: Churchill And His Money* (2015).

Bibliography

Augustine of Hippo. *Enchiridion* (Regnery, 2002).
Baker, John R. *Race* (Ostara, 2016).
Bernays, Edward. *Propaganda* (Ig Publishing, 2005).
Bhagavad Gita (Collier, 1972). Translated by A.C. Bhaktivedanta Swami Prabhupada.
Bolton, Kerry. *Yockey* (Arktos, 2018).
Bradberry, Benton. *The Myth of German Villainy* (AuthorHouse, 2012).
Buber, Martin.
    – *I And Thou* (Touchstone, 1996).
    – *Kingship of God* (Harper & Row, 1967).
Bundesarchiv Berlin NS 22/27 (18 January 1941), "Über personelle Auswertung der Schulung zur Personalpolitik."
Byman, Daniel. "Riots, white supremacy, and accelerationism" (Brookings Institute, 02 June 2020).
Dalton, Thomas.
    – *Classic Essays on the Jewish Question* (ed., Clemens & Blair, 2022).
    – *Goebbels on the Jews* (Castle Hill, 2019).
    – *Hitler on the Jews* (Castle Hill, 2019).
    – *Protocols of the Elders of Zion: The Definitive English Edition* (Clemens & Blair, 2023).
    – *The Jewish Hand in the World Wars* (Castle Hill, 2019).
Dares the Phrygian. *The Trojan War* (Modern Library, 1966).
Devi, Savitri. *Gold in the Furnace* (1952).
Döhring, Herbert. *Living with Hitler* (Greenhill Books, 2018).
Evola, Julius. *Men Among the Ruins* (Inner Traditions, 2002).
Feuerbach, Ludwig. *The Essence of Christianity* (Mineola, 2008).
Friedrich, Martin.
    – *Hitler Avatāra* (Clemens & Blair, 2023),
    – *Myth and Sun: Essays of the* Archetype (Clemens & Blair, 2022).
Garrett, Henry.
    – *Children: Black & White* (Patrick Henry Press, 1967).
    – *IQ and Racial Differences* (Noontide Press, 1980).
Goebbels, Joseph. *Goebbels: Articles and Speeches, 1927-1945* (Digital Archive).
Gregor, A. James. *Origins and Doctrine of Fascism* (Transaction Publishers, 2005).

Herf, Jeffrey. *Reactionary Modernism: Technology, Culture, and Politics in Weimar and the Third Reich* (Cambridge University Press, 1990).
Hesiod, *Works and Days* (Harvard University Press, 1914).
Hess, Wolf Rüdiger. *My Father Rudolf Hess* (Star, 1987).
Hitler, Adolf.
- *Complete Speeches, 1922-1945* (Digital Archive).
- *Mein Kampf* (Wewelsburg Archives, 2018).
- *Mein Kampf*, English-German, vols. 1 & 2 (Clemens & Blair, 2017).

Homer, *Iliad*.
International Court of Justice (Nuremberg Trial Archives, 2018).
Johnson, Greg. "Against Accelerationism" (Counter Currents, 06 January 2020).
Johnson, M. Raphael. *The Barnes Review* (July/August 2001), "The Tragedy of Rudolf Hess: What Kind of Man was He?"
Jung, Carl. *The Archetypes and the Collective Unconscious* (Princeton University Press, 1969).
Jünger, Ernst.
- *On Pain* (Telos Press, 2008).
- *The Worker* (Northwestern University Press, 2017).
- *Die Standarte*.
  - "Differentiation and Connection" (September 1925).
  - "The Frontline Soldier" (September 1925).
  - "The Machine" (December 1925).
  - "Blood" (April 1926).
  - "Nationalist Revolution" (20 May 1926).
  - "Unite!" (June 1926).
- *Widerstand*. "On Spirit" (April 1927).
- *Völkischer Beobachter*. "Revolution and the Idea" (September 1923).

Kaczynski, Ted.
- *Industrial Society and Its Future* (Digital Archive).
- *Unabomber In His Own Words* (2020), part 3.

Kant, Immanuel. *Critique of Pure Reason*, "Transcendental Doctrine of Judgment."
Kierkegaard, Søren.
- *Fear and Trembling* (Princeton University Press, 1983).
- *Philosophical Fragments* (Princeton University Press, 1987).
- *Purity of Heart is to Will One Thing* (Harper, 1956).
- *Training in Christianity* (Vintage, 2004).

Khomeini, Ruhollah. *Islamic Government: Governance of the Jurist*. Translated by H. Algar.

Lauterpacht, Hersch. *British Year Book of International Law* (1944), "The Law of Nations and Punishment of War Crimes."
Ley, Robert. *Pesthauch der Welt* (Müller Verlag, 1944).
Loadenthal, Michael. "Feral fascists and deep green guerrillas: infrastructural attack and accelerationist terror," *Critical Studies on Terrorism*, 15:1 (2022).
Lough, David. *No More Champagne: Churchill And His Money* (Head of Zeus, 2015).
Louis, William Roger. *The Oxford History of the British Empire: The Eighteenth Century* (Oxford University Press, 1998).
Lynn, Richard. *Race Differences in Intelligence* (Washington Summit, 2015).
Magun, Artemy. "Karl Marx and Hannah Arendt on the Jewish Question: Political Theology as a Critique," *Continental Philosophy Review* 45, no. 4 (2012).
Malloy, Jason. National Library of Medicine. National Institutes of Health. "James Watson tells the inconvenient truth: faces the consequences" (April 2008).
Marx, Karl. "On the Jewish Question" (1844).
Melaouhi, Abdallah. *Rudolf Hess: His Murder and Betrayal* (TBR, 2013).
Mommsen, Theodor. *The History of Rome* (1856/1871).
Murray, Charles. *The Bell Curve* (Free Press, 1994).
Nietzsche, Friedrich.
  - *On the Genealogy of Morals*. Translated by Horace B. Samuel.
  - *Joyful Science*. Translated by Thomas Common.
  - *The Will to Power*. Translated by Anthony Ludovici.
  - *Thus Spoke Zarathustra*. Translated by Thomas Common.
Orchard, Andy. *Dictionary of Norse Myth and Legend* (Cassell, 1997).
Ovid, *Metamorphoses* (published as *Tales From Ovid*, Farrar, 1998). Translated by Ted Hughes.
Parker, DeWitt. *Schopenhauer Selections* (Scribner, 1928).
Parsons, Howard. *The Journal of Religion* 44, no. 1 (1964), "The Prophetic Mission of Karl Marx."
Pine, Lisa. *History of Education* (2014), vol. 43, no. 2, "The NS-Ordensburgen: training for political leadership."
Plaim, Anna, Döhring, Herman. *Living with Hitler* (Greenhill Books, 2018).
Poetic Edda (Princeton University Press, 1936). Translated by H.A. Bellows.
Rassinier, Paul. *The Real Eichmann Trial* (IHR, 2002).

Rauschning, Hermann.
- *Germany's Revolution of Destruction* (Heinemann, 1940).
- *The Voice of Destruction* (Putnam, 1940).

Rochelson, Meri-Jane. *A Jew in the Public Arena* (Wayne State University Press, 2008).

Sack, John. *Eye for an Eye* (Basic Books, 1993).

Schmitt, Carl. *Political Theology* (University of Chicago Press, 2005).

Schopenhauer, Arthur. *Parerga and Paralipomena,* volume two (Oxford University Press, 1974).

Serrano, Miguel.
- *Adolf Hitler: The Ultimate Avatar* (Hermitage Helm, 2014).
- *Hitler's UFO Against the New World Order* (55 Club, 2016).
- *Manu: For the Man to Come* (Hermitage Helm, 2017).
- *NOS: Book of the Resurrection* (Routledge, 1984).
- *Resurrection of the Hero* (55 Club, 2015).

Spengler, Oswald.
- *Man and Technics* (Knopf, 1963).
- *The Decline of the West* (Vintage Books, 2006).
- *The Hour of Decision* (University Press of the Pacific, 2002).

Stein, Ben. *The View From Sunset Boulevard* (Basic Books, 1979).

Tacitus, *Complete Works of Tacitus* (Random House, 1942).

The International Court of Justice: custodian of the archives of the International Military Tribunal at Nuremberg (Nuremberg Trial Archives, 2018).

Thomas, W. Hugh. *The Murder of Rudolf Hess* (Harper & Row, 1979).

Trotsky, Leon. *The Revolution Betrayed* (Dover, 2004).

Upanishads, The (Penguin, 1965).

van den Bruck, Arthur Möller. *Das Dritte Reich* (Arktos, 2012).

Wagner, Richard. *Deutsche Kunst und Deutsche Politik* (1867).

Yockey, Francis Parker. *Imperium* (Westropa, 1948).

www.ingramcontent.com/pod-product-compliance
Ingram Content Group UK Ltd.
Pitfield, Milton Keynes, MK11 3LW, UK
UKHW061624240426
12049UKWH00028B/130